ARCHAEOLOGY IS A BRAND!

THE MEANING OF ARCHAEOLOGY IN CONTEMPORARY POPULAR CULTURE

Cornelius Holtorf

ILLUSTRATED BY
Quentin Drew

Left
Coast
Press
inc.

Walnut Creek, CA

Published in North America by:
  Left Coast Press, Inc.
  1630 N Main Street #400
  Walnut Creek, CA 94596
  www.LCoastPress.com

Published in the rest of the world by: Archaeopress, Gordon House, 276 Banbury Road,
  Oxford OX2 7ED England, www.archaeopress.com

Library of Congress Cataloging-in-Publication Data

  Holtorf, Cornelius, 1968-
  Archaeology is a brand : the meaning of archaeology in contemporary popular culture /
  Cornelius Holtorf ; illustrated by Quentin Drew.
      p. cm.
  Includes bibliographical references and index.
  ISBN 978-1-59874-178-0 (hardback : alk. paper)
  ISBN 978-1-59874-179-7 (pbk. : alk. paper)
  1. Archaeology--Social aspects. 2. Popular cul-
  ture--Great Britain. 3. Popular culture--Germany.
  4. Popular culture--Sweden. 5. Popular culture--
  United States. 6. Mass media--Social aspects. 7.
  Archaeology--Public opinion. 8. Archaeologists--
  Public opinion. I. Title.
      CC175.H65 2007   930.1--dc22
          2007001955

The paper used in this publication meets the minimum
requirements of the American National Standard for
Information Sciences—Permanence of Paper for
Printed Library Materials, ANSI/NISO Z39.48-1992 (R
1997) (Permanenc

09 10 5 4 3 2

"Insofar as archaeology enhances people's lives and society in general, its major impact might be said to lie in popular culture rather than any noble vision of improving self-awareness."

Gavin Lucas (2004: 119)

Table of contents

Preface

This book is about the meaning of archaeology in contemporary popular culture. It is not a manual for improving the public understanding of the discipline of archaeology. There will be important lessons for professional archaeology to be learned, but these lie on a more general level than specific methods and approaches applicable to individual public education initiatives.

Many archaeologists use the term "archaeology" indiscriminately to refer both to their own field or subject and to the past being studied, for example in the book title *The Archaeology of Britain: An Introduction from the Upper Palaeolithic to the Industrial Revolution* and in the magazine title *Archäologie in Deutschland*. I do not. This book is concerned with the meaning of the field or subject of archaeology only. I am not disputing the great significance of popular representations of the past but they have not been the topic of my research.

I will be presenting important facts, analyses and interpretations and a few potentially controversial arguments about the social role of archaeology. My intended audience is professional archaeologists and others working in the (broadly defined) heritage sector as well as students studying fields such as archaeology, heritage, cultural studies or science studies. The book will also be relevant to all those interested in the field that has become known as the "public understanding of science" and in studies of the depiction of science and scientists in popular culture.

It's not just archaeology,
its an adventure!

Acknowledgments

The research presented in this work was conducted while I held a Marie Curie Fellowship of the European Commission at the Swedish National Heritage Board (*Riksantikvarieämbetet*) in Stockholm, Sweden. All views presented and not directly attributed to others are mine alone and I bear sole responsibility for the content of this work.

A very large number of people have assisted me during my research with various queries, made many valuable suggestions, and some permitted me also to cite from their email messages to me. I would like to thank them all:

Peter Alexander-Fitzgerald, Morintz Alexandru, Stefan Altekamp, Tanya Armbrüster, Karin Arvastson, Neal Ascherson, Cissi Askwall, Håkan Aspeborg, Rainer Atzbach, Michele C. Aubry, Kirsty Ayling, Josep Ballart, Paul Barford, Laszlo Bartosiewicz, Jane E. Baxter, Mary Beaudry, Colleen Beck, Marion Benz, Ewa Bergdahl, Diane Bjorklund, Rui Boaventura, René Bräunig, Mats Burström, Günter Buuck, Deborah Cannon, Tom Carlsson, Geoff Carver, Alejandro Chu, Anita Cohen-Williams, Marvin Cohodas, Cerridwen Connelly, Michael A. Cremo, Sarah Cross, Anton Cruysheer, Chris Cumberpatch, Linda Scott Cummings, Anka Dawid, Tim Darvill, Eric Deetz, Kathryn Denning, Heidrun Derks, Kurt D'Haens, Erik Dobat, Marcia-Anne Dobres, David Ebert, Ernestine Elster, Corinna Endlich, Chris Evans, Graham Fairlough, Jason Fancher, Harald Fäth, Kathrin Felder, Svante Fischer, Adam Fish, Lena Flodin, Meredith Fraser, Ingrid Fuglestvedt, Amy Gazin-Schwartz, Duane Gehlsen, Björn Gesemann, Joel Gilman, Anne Katrine Gjerløff, Alice Gorman, Roman Grabolle, Göran Gruber, Jonas Grundberg, Mirko Gutjahr, Alejandro Haber, Per Hœrnes, Graham Hancock, Meredith Hardy, David Harris, David Haskiya, Henning Haßmann, Christoph Heiermann, Regina Heilmann, Heather Henderson, Suzanne Hendriks, Don Henson, Carl Heron, Mike Heyworth, Matthew Hill, Louise Hitchcock, Ian Hodder, Jan Hoff, Anders Högberg, Ingunn Holm, Nadia Z. Iacono, Gyles Iannone, Ulf Ickerodt, Malin Ideland, Sarah Jennings, Gerson Jeute, Matthew Johnson, Sarah Johnson, Desmond Johnston, Catarina Karlsson, Jean Kelly, Renee Kennedy-Martin, Marco Kirchner, Ingela Kishonti, Ivan Kisjes, Kerstin Kowarik, Troels Myrup Kristensen, Karol Kulik, Nicola Laneri, Josara de Lange, Maia Marie Langley, Joseph I. Lauer, Cherry Lavell, Garry Law, Joanne Lea, Juliane Lippok, Barbara Little, Johannes Litzel, Lilia Lizama, Troy Lovata, Gavin Lucas, Leanne Mallory, Hans Manneby, Ingo Marzahn, Thomas Mathis, Carol McDavid, David Meadows, Krissy

Moore, Lawrence E. Moore, Robert Muckle, Jan Mulder, Ymke Mulder, Marcus Müller, Hansjürgen Müller-Beck, Carol A. Nickolai, Catalin Nicolae, Gerard Niemoeller, Bengt Nordqvist, Johan Normark, Joan Oates, David Oels, Eric Olijdam, Atle Omland, Gilbert Oteyo, Sven Ouzman, Petra Pansegrau, Jeanne Pepalis, Bodil Petersson, Caroline Phillips, Angela Piccini, Nancy Pinto-Orton, David Pokotylo, Peter Prestel, Christine Prior, Paul Probst, Lyndel V. Prott, Anne Pyburn, Patricia Rahemipour, Carolyn Rauh, Elliot Richmond, Simone Riehl, Steve Rosen, Ian A. Russell, Miles Russell, Vince Russett, Alun Salt, Stefanie Samida, Catrin Sandberg, Fabio Sani, Beth Savage, Diane Scherzler, Andrea Schlickmann, Matt Schlitz, Martin Schmidt, George Schneider, Astrid Schoonhoven, Andrew Selkirk, Jan Selmer, Stefan Seufert, Andrew R. Sewell, Michael Shanks, Kristín Huld Sigurðardóttir, George S. Smith, Stuart T Smith, Björn Magnusson Staaf, Jody N. Steele, Christoph Steinacker, Tom Stern, Adam Stout, Jimmy Strassburg, Iain Stuart, Suzanne Thompson-Wright, Viktor Trifonov, Dries Tys, Jonna Ulin, Robyn Veal, Katty Hauptmann Wahlgren, Joe Watkins, Ethan Watrall, Douglas Watt, David Webb, Stig Welinder, Clark Wernecke, Laure West, Jes Wienberg, Willem Willems, Bob Wishoff, Robyn Woodward, Mareile Wulf, Christiane Zintzen, Sultana Zorpidu.

I am particularly grateful to all those who took the time to talk to me at length about specific topics in relation to my research. They include Peter Addyman, Jonathan Bateman, Göran Burenhult, Mike Heyworth, Magnus Krantz, Jesper Ohlsson, Francis Pryor, Gunter Schöbel, Henrik Summanen and John Walker.

Special thanks are due to Ingrid Pfeiffer in Bremen, who heard about my project and undertook her own survey to assist me, and to Karen D Vitelli and her students Wendy Eliason, Justin Franklin, Emily Freund and Betsey Wiegman in the Spring 2003 Archaeological Ethics class of the Department of Anthropology at Indiana University, USA, who supported my research through a video montage entitled *Dinosaurs, Dullards and Danger: Representations of Archaeology in Popular Culture*.

Over the past few years, various audiences at conferences and workshops in Stockholm, Uppsala, Washington, DC, St. Petersburg, Härnosand, Skara, Berlin and Lund, at University Departments in Vienna, Stockholm, Berlin, Bristol, Tübingen, and Helsingborg, at Upplands Museum in Uppsala and within my (then) own institution, the Swedish National Heritage Board, in Stockholm and Mölndal gave me opportunities to discuss parts of my work and receive valuable feedback. I would also like to thank my colleagues at the Swedish National Heritage Board in Stockholm, many of whom helped

with suggestions and comments over the two years I was based there to conduct my research.

All or parts of this manuscript have been read by Ewa Bergdahl, Tom Carlsson, David Davison, Göran Gruber, Håkan Karlsson, Karol Kulik, Björn Magnusson Staaf, Nick Merriman, Bodil Petersson, George S. Smith and Tom Stern and I am grateful to them all for their suggestions.

My greatest thanks is to Quentin Drew, the artist, archaeologist, and teacher at the Department of Archaeology and Anthropology, University of Wales, Lampeter. He was keen from the start to illustrate this book, putting his own spin on the issues discussed. Quentin understands better than most that archaeology is supposed to be fun!

It has become customary for authors, especially men, to apologise for the evenings, weekends and holidays which they used to write the book rather than spend with their families. The following disclaimer is thus in order. Families have not been harmed during the researching, writing and editing of this book.

I dedicate this book to the memory of Arne who died as the first draft of this book had just been completed and to his grand daughter Melanie who was born the following year. Unlike her older brother Tom, she still lives a simple life with simple pleasures, and is quite unaware of the fantastic science of archaeology.

PS. All URLs mentioned in this book were current on 28 March 2006 unless another date is given.

Chapter 1

Investigating the meaning of archaeology in popular culture

The summer is the time for archaeological excavations. Every year, thousands of excavations are taking place all over Europe and beyond. A very large proportion of them is rescue archaeology, i.e. projects that aim at rescuing information from ancient sites before they get destroyed through development. In most Western countries, developers are required by law to pay for the costs of these excavations. Professional archaeology has until recently been a field that defined itself nearly exclusively in relatively narrow academic terms. But now that both states and many businesses are in difficult economic situations, professional archaeologists feel an increasing need to justify what they are doing for society. Is it still right that tax-payers and consumers should be paying for research concerning the distant past? Do archaeologists have social responsibilities and duties beyond contributing to academic enlightenment?

The ensuing process of "opening up" archaeology to take into account broader social contexts has, however, not only been forced upon the subject from the outside. A quickly expanding interest in a wide range of issues and phenomena that have come to be known as "public archaeology" is fundamentally transforming even the academic discipline itself (Merriman 2002). For example, a few years ago, a new academic journal called *Public Archaeology* was founded with the express purpose "to analyse and report on archaeological and heritage issues which relate to the wider world of politics, ethics, government, social questions, education, management, economics and philosophy".[1] All these elements taken together describe the field within which professional archaeology is operating today.

"it's our money sonny
and we want some answers.....
- where are the receipts?
- where are the budget plans?
- where are the goods?"

---

[1] http://www.jxj.com/parch

The meaning of archaeology in popular culture is a topic born out of that same opening process of the discipline of archaeology, manifesting the trend towards a truly public archaeology. It is not surprising that others too have found the contemporary image of the archaeologist an interesting field of study. For example, a group of archaeology students at Humboldt University in Berlin conducted extensive research about "Indy, Lara and Hercule – how the media determine the image of the archaeologist" (Felder et al 2003). Their results were presented in an exhibition shown in their university (13 March – 3 April 2003). A wide range of topical examples from fictional literature, movies and computer games, was thoroughly analysed and categorised. Among other topics, the group considered the discrepancy between the depiction of archaeology and its reality and asked whether actual archaeological practice influenced the existing clichés and to which extent those determine the public expectations of professional archaeology.

Elsewhere, another group of students prepared an exhibition entitled "From Heinrich Schliemann to Lara Croft. The Fascination of the Past" which was shown in Freiburg's University Library (20 May –18 June 2003):

> "'The past? That exists only in history books anyway!' – 'False!', say those responsible for this exhibition. In fact, we encounter the past in many realms of our lives in which we may not suspect it. Whether in TV, in advertisements or while shopping: we come across the relics of ancient peoples everywhere [...] This is similar in relation to the discipline of Archaeology. It does not only supply us with these witnesses of the past but in recent years, it has also attracted increasing interest among the media. This exhibition is intended to demonstrate that archaeologists are not dealing with periods that are long past and far removed from us – in other words, periods that do not need to mean anything to us. Quite the opposite: the relics of various different, lost civilizations are more present and have a larger impact today than ever before. [...]"[2]

My own two-year long investigations about the meaning and portrayal of archaeology in contemporary popular culture were conducted as part of a larger research focus on "Archaeology in Society" which the Swedish National Heritage Board devoted particular attention to over recent years. One of its main aims has been to adapt the practice of Swedish cultural heritage management to changing social conditions, by re-evaluating its practices and seeking out new opportunities.

---

[2] http://www.ub.uni-freiburg.de/ausstellung/2003-05-20/index.html (my translation)

A path-breaking initiative carried out across the entire Swedish heritage sector over three years fits into this context, too. Entitled *Agenda Kulturarv* (best translated as *Operation Heritage*), this grand project was about putting the social significance of the cultural heritage on the agenda of a broad discussion between many stake-holders within the Swedish heritage sector. Its aim was to refine professional practice in order to make the most of people's interest in the past and the cultural heritage and to make the work of the professionals accessible and relevant to them.[3] The manifesto that resulted from the project (Agenda Kulturarv 2004) resolved that all people in society should be enabled and encouraged to draw on the power of archaeological sites, as a part of the cultural heritage more generally. That power was said to be twofold. Stories about the past told in relation to the heritage could (a) broaden peoples' perspectives on the present and (b) create familiar surroundings that make people at home. As far as historical perspectives on the present are concerned, I imagine that they could be based either on actual hard knowledge about the laws, patterns or trends of history, or on softer insights about the variety of different human realities. The question is, however, how much archaeological research, focussing on inconclusive evidence about limited aspects of societies that existed a long time ago, can really contribute to any such results.

The fact that many people state, when asked, that they are interested in the past, find archaeology exciting and enjoy visiting excavations (see chapter 4) is not really helpful in deciding the question about the social benefits gained from archaeology. After all, Erich von Däniken's new theme park in Switzerland, called Mystery Park[4] and his numerous books about archaeological topics have been popular too (see chapter 5). I am inclined to concur with Gavin Lucas (2004: 119) who argued that insofar as archaeology enhances people's lives and society in general, its major impact might be said to lie in popular culture rather than in any noble vision of improving self-awareness through "historical perspectives". What this actually means, is the topic of the present book.

Archaeology: a trendy subject

In order to get a better grip on people's fascination with archaeology in popular culture, it is useful to consult studies that describe larger, underlying trends in Western culture and society. Over a decade ago, the German sociologist Gerhard Schulze (1993) published

---

[3] http://www.agendakulturarv.se
[4] http://www.mysterypark.ch

a study describing *Die Erlebnisgesellschaft* (The Experience Society). In this book, which has been very influential in the German social sciences, Schulze argued that *Erlebniswert* (experience value) is quickly replacing use and monetary values in significance. As people in affluent Western societies have become economically secure and possess all the tools they require, they are orientating their lives more and more towards experiences: to live and to experience have nearly come to mean the same thing. Whereas in the past you may have received a book or a mobile phone as birthday presents, now you are almost more likely to get a bungee jump or a day on an excavation (see chapter 2)! As a consequence, the market for experiences is expanding fast. The Swedish geographer Orvar Löfgren (1999: 16) cautioned that this is not an entirely new trend but has roots that go at least two centuries back: tourism has always been largely about experiences. Yet today, from travel agencies to shopping centres, from TV stations to universities and from swimming pools to theme parks, all are offering experiences to their customers (see also Köck 1990: 77-82; Pine and Gilmore 1999; Schmitt 1999; O'Dell 2002).

The difficult choices people are facing when having to choose between competing experiences are often, albeit unconsciously, informed by larger social patterns. Whereas some sections of the population prefer experiences such as listening to classical music and contemplating art in museums, others enjoy *schlager* music and watching sentimental films on TV and others again like rock'n roll, pub visits and generally "action" (Schulze 1993: 142-57). Companies trying to reach certain groups of consumers have long understood the significance of framing their products within existing patterns of differently favoured experiences. Similarly, customers prefer to buy products that relate to the preferred experiences of those people as which they see themselves (Schulze 1993: chapter 9). This might explain, at least in parts, why the "product" archaeology enjoys the amount of popularity it does. It offers and is perceived to offer, valued experiences for many. Visiting an archaeological museum or excavation site can be about ancient art and education about the past, about usually idyllic reconstructions of past daily life and re-assurance about one's home village, or about modern computer technology and quests for treasure in the spirit of Indiana Jones who is probably the best known archaeologist in the world today (Bahn 1989: 59). In each case, it is a particular experience in the present that accounts for peoples' interest in the past.

At about the same time when Schulze wrote his book, the American marketing "guru" Faith Popcorn published *The Popcorn Report* (1992) in which she predicted certain trends for the future. She recommended to companies to "bend" their products around such trends. One of the ten most important trends she noticed was a trend towards "fantasy

adventure" which she described as "a momentary, wild-and-crazy retreat from the world into an exotic flavour" (Popcorn 1992: 34). Popcorn's prediction was that product appeal will increasingly result from offering the safe and familiar with adventurous, exotic or sensual twists. Again, archaeology seems predestined to play a key role. What could be more safe and familiar yet at the same time adventurous, exotic and sensual than a visit to an archaeological excavation site or museum near your own home, where archaeologists, the "cowboys of science" (Holtorf 2005: 42), tell you about peoples' lives in

Archaeology in Call of Cthulhu – a conversation with Jesper Ohlsson

Call of Cthulhu (CoC) is a classic role-playing game, first published in 1981 by Chaosium. The game has sold over 300,000 copies worldwide and won dozens of game-industry awards. Its underlying story about the *Cthulhu Mythos*, an alternative version of our own universe, was inspired by the horror stories of the American writer H. P. Lovecraft (1890 – 1937). Evil godlike beings, banished from earth millions of years ago, are slowly returning to a world now dominated by us humans. Most people are unaware of this fact. But those few who still possess knowledge about ancient myth and history are beginning to understand what has been going on. They start to look for ways to fight the monstrous creatures...

CH: *How significant is archaeology in CoC adventures?*

JO: Archaeology plays an important role in the CoC game. Archaeology is one of the tools a player character might use in order to find clues for how to stop the creatures from entering our world. In fact, scholarly skills are at times more important than gun wielding and swordplay which otherwise tend to dominate role-playing games. Add to this the fact that ancient artefacts and historical documents of all kinds often play a vital part in the adventures.

CH: *What is it that makes archaeologists attractive characters in CoC adventures?*

JO: When you create a player character you have to choose a profession for the character. According to the rule book, each profession has a specified list of possible skills. Since scholarly skills are very useful, players often choose academic professions for their characters. The most romantic and best known type of scholar in popular fiction is probably the adventurous Indiana Jones and many choose to play with archaeologists based on that model. Of course, archaeology in this game world is far from what archaeology is all about in the real world, but it is fun to play with clichés and stereotypes.

CH: *Thank you, Jesper.*

[Jesper Ohlsson is a school teacher living in Stockholm. He has been into role-playing games since he was in his early teens. He has also been active in an archaeological project on Gotland. His own CoC role play homepage is at http://members.tripod.com/~Jeppan/CoC.html.]

the past? At the Experimental Centre at Lejre[5] in Denmark you can even book an entire family holiday entitled "Living in the past" (Köck 1990: 69). Archaeology can have a lot in common with fantasy adventure.

When the German leisure expert Horst Opaschowski (2000) recently reviewed these trends, he found that the "Experience industry" was still expanding. Opaschoswki made the additional point that this industry is essentially telling fairytales and selling dreams rather than products. What mattered more than the veracity and authenticity of these tales and dreams was that they create the right sensual experiences and thus customer satisfaction. More generally, the American economists Joseph Pine and James Gilmore argued in their book *The Experience Economy* (1999: 25) that those "businesses that relegate themselves to the diminishing world of goods and services will be rendered irrelevant." Instead, businesses now need to offer experiences to people. These experiences consist of more than entertainment and are first and foremost about *engaging* people sensually, cognitively, socially, culturally and emotionally. How to do just that is developed with examples in the economist Bernd H. Schmitt's account of *Experiential Marketing* (1999).

In his account of *The Dream Society* (1999), the Danish marketing consultant Rolf Jensen[6] took this discussion further. Going beyond the previously mentioned studies, Jensen argued that consumers are now increasingly buying stories along with products. For example, when we buy eggs we are willing to pay a little more in order to hear a story about free-ranging chicken. Likewise, we are prepared to donate money to Amnesty International or Greenpeace because (besides everything else they do) they tell us stories about rescuing human beings or natural environments that we respond to very passionately. By the same token, advertising is becoming more emotional, appealing to our hearts rather than our brains (see also Klein 2001; Jensen 2002).

Some emotional stories have, of course, been with us for considerable time. They include stories about nations, political ideologies and state religions. Although few archaeologists are proud of it, in the past they have been making significant contributions to each of these grand stories (see e.g. Kohl and Fawcett 1995). Indeed, the size and status of many contemporary archaeological institutions as well as the strong legal protection of archaeological heritage in the Western world owe a lot to the very firm and long-

---

[5] http://www.lejre-center.dk
[6] http://www.dreamcompany.dk

standing links between archaeology and stories about the origins of modern nations. Only relatively recently has a focus on the *national* heritage been replaced by one on the *cultural* heritage.

Now, new kinds of stories are emerging that are particularly characteristic for the *Dream Society* in which, according to Jensen, we will be living in the future. All of them provide experiences by engaging us in different ways. Three out of the six main stories of Jensen's *Dream Society* can be told, in parts, through archaeology (the other three are Togetherness, friendship and love; Who-Am-I; and Convictions). These stories are about

(a) Adventures (see also Köck 1990): archaeology is particularly good at telling adventure stories, usually based around its fieldwork. Significantly, Rolf Jensen

- "...... and there in the section below
context two-seven-four was found
the fabled, but cursed roof tile of
Mullbury manor! All those who have catalogued
this evil artifact have since perished mysteriously."

OLD
POTS
£1

himself is seen on his web pages as sitting at a desk with an *Indiana Jones* film poster on the wall behind him. It proclaims *The return of the great adventure*.

(b) Care: in the *Dream Society*, people have an increased need to provide care. They like caring for pets, save whales from extinction and donate money towards humanitarian aid in emergencies. Zoos, once doomed, are popular again because they present themselves as conservation centres. Likewise, significant parts of professional archaeology have in recent years redefined themselves in terms of preservation. Archaeology is now often presented as being about managing ancient sites or artefacts as non-renewable resources and rescuing precious finds and evidence, in a race against time, from obliteration due to modern development.

(c) Peace of Mind: in an insecure and constantly changing world, people desire peace of mind and reassurance in relation to their livelihoods, ways of life and values. They seek answers rather than more questions. They like romanticizing the past and trust established brands more than new products. Among the themes which established brands draw on are stereotypical sceneries of the past and, in a way, they in turn have become archaeological brands. Jensen's examples include the world of Classical Greece featuring shining temples with Doric columns and philosophers immersed in discussion on the market square. He also refers to the Scandinavian

8

Vikings who venture out in their longboats to plunder foreign shores, yet preserve their purity of mind. Peace of mind can also be evoked by stories that extend our own daily routines back into the distant past. A recent Swedish newspaper report, for example, was entitled "Commuters in the Stone Age" (*Helsingborgs Dagblad*, 25 October 2002, my translation). The ubiquitous celebration of origins provides reassurance in an insecure present.

These books I have been referring to are not brand-new. Yet much of what they are about seems to be very relevant still today. If Schulze, Pine and Gilmore, Opaschowski, Popcorn and Jensen are broadly correct in their analyses, this is an age in which archaeology should do particularly well. Indeed, already during the 1960s, the German archaeologist Horst Kirchner (1964: 5) suggested that the 20th century would become known as "the great century of archaeology". The Swiss historian Franz Georg Maier (1981) referred two decades later to an evident "archaeomania" in Western culture. Concerning the last decade, Karol Kulik argued that we have been living through a "golden age" of archaeology in the mass media (see chapter 3). Historical reconstructions and re-enactments of various kinds are very popular attractions in the Dream Society, not just in Sweden (Aronsson and Larsson 2002). In the year 1999-2000, history and archaeology books reportedly outsold cookery books in the U.K. (Paynton 2002: 44). Moreover, since 1996 the archaeology-inspired computer game series *Tomb Raider* featuring Lara Croft sold in millions worldwide, each game topping the PlayStation game best-seller lists. The first associated feature film grossed more than $274 million worldwide (Rose 2003).

Clearly, archaeology is no longer a subject that only small sections of the population find interesting. Archaeology is today a popular theme in many genres and formats of popular culture (see Appendix 1). Although this popularity may have grown out of an archaeo-appeal the subject has perhaps always had (Daniel 1964: chapter 8; Pallottino 1968; Andreae 1981; Zintzen 1998; Russell 2002a), it certainly reached new peaks in recent years (Jensen and Wieczorek 2002). According to one prediction for the US, archaeology will become even more popular when the baby boom generation is going to retire after about 2010. As part of the expected upswing of the leisure industry, the American archaeologist Lawrence Moore (2006) predicts the emergence of "Recreation Archaeology" as a subset of Public Archaeology. Recreation Archaeology customises archaeology to the public and maximises public appeal. According to this analysis, Recreation Archaeology will eventually be succeeding Cultural Resource Management (CRM) as the main focus of the discipline in society.

OLD POTS £1

A digging hymn was written by Pete Townshend of *The Who* for the musical *The Ironman* from 1989. Entitled "Dig", the song suggests that when you are sick and afraid of some danger, you should grab "a pick and a spade" in order dig a burial mound for "the beast". Removed from light and sound, digging in the ground – according to the song – promises your life

      salvation
            protection
                  release
                        resurrection
                              peace
                                  pleasure
                                      pride
                                          treasure
                                              stones
                                                  metal
                                                      bones.

It is a truly beautiful digging song, which Stefan Seufert first made me aware of. Had we received permission, we would have quoted some of the lyrics here. They are also available at http://www.sing365.com.

The public appeal of archaeology does however lie on a different level than professional archaeologists – pleased by the interest in their work – often assume. Archaeology provides memorable experiences which fascinate many people. It tells stories that relate to wider trends and themes of our society. It is practically engaging people in various ways. Many of these experiences, stories and engagements draw on the practices of *doing* archaeology in the present: excavating ancient remains, discovering "treasures", rescuing archaeological sites and investigating our origins with the help of modern technology loom large. When it refers back to the past, much archaeological appeal derives from idealized clichés that are nothing but our own visions superimposed on times gone by. In each case, it appears that the meaning of archaeology in society is more to do with metaphors and stereotypes than with literal truth about the past (see also chapter 5).

From a purely academic point of view, this conclusion may be seen as sad and deeply unsettling. But humans have always drawn on a rich supply of metaphors and prejudices that provided guidance and visions for their lives. Arguably, the world is too complex for

everybody to assess all of it on its own merits. Social psychologists have long understood that every society and every age needs to provide specific "short-cuts" for making the unfamiliar familiar (Moscovici 1984).

The British archaeologist Julian Thomas argued in his book *Archaeology and Modernity* (2004) that the discipline of archaeology is intrinsically linked to a modernist worldview. It could only have been generated in the specific context of the modern world and is firmly tied to the conditions of modernity as they developed over the past few centuries in the Western world. A similar argument has been made by the Swedish archaeologist Björn Magnusson Staaf (2000) regarding the defining influence of modernism on archaeological heritage management and research design. As the modern world and its conditions are now changing beyond recognition, both Thomas (2004: 223) and Staaf (2000: 192) wonder whether that means that scientific archaeology and heritage management, too, will need to change in order to remain relevant. As the German journalist and archaeological author Dieter Kapff (2004: 130) put it in a recent commentary:

> "Archaeology appeals to a large number of people. But members of the contemporary fun-society are not actually interested in increasing their knowledge, in education, information or intellectual stimuli. The educated classes [Bildungsbürgertum] of the 19th and early 20th centuries no longer exist. Today, people want entertainment." (my translation)

Does, then, a new type of society require a new profile for archaeology? Have the links between archaeology and traditional values of education been cut? Is the popular portrayal of archaeology indicating archaeology's own future? Already now, popular archaeology contributes to some of the themes and stories that increasingly give orientation and quality of life to people today. But as things stand, computer game manufacturers, Hollywood studios and entrepreneurs like von Däniken benefit most from the currency of archaeological themes.

As society transforms itself, archaeologists need to know precisely what it is that almost everybody else seems to find so irresistible about "their" subject. They also need to ask themselves where they wish to position their subject, their own profession and the role of their institutions in relation to that existing appeal. In the light of a number of particular significant key themes that have come to define the subject of archaeology in the popular domain, the entire field may need to be rethought – and certainly the way, archaeologists themselves have been relating to their popular representations. This kind

"Meanwhile, The Wop had discovered that the piper and violinist on either side of him were not, as he had suspected, Bearded Wristy Intellectuals, but, respectively, a plumber and a builder who happened to have been brought up to play pipes and violins as well.
—Are the beards compulsory? he asked the piper, with his regulation aggressiveness.
—They pretty well are for touring in Germany, the piper replied, unoffended. —You into this archaeology too?
—No, fuck, replied The Wop, mistakenly aligning himself to the assumed mindset of an English plumber in an English pub.
—No? Oh. Jesus, I think it's great stuff. Always used to love chatting to Harry about it. Nothing like a bit of education to improve the evening.
—Oh, said The Wop. Then he fell silent, hopelessly confused by this representative of a non-anti-intellectual blokedom."

From James Hawes' novel **Dead Long Enough** (2001: 113)

of analysis is not entirely original but increasingly shared even by senior representatives of the discipline. For example, Brian Fagan, the doyen of American archaeology, recently stated (2002: 255, 258):

"Today's archaeology requires new skills, new sensitivities for communicating effectively with the wider audience [...]. We are woefully unprepared for the challenges of an entirely new kind of archaeology. ... The academic culture is becoming increasingly irrelevant to much of what contemporary archaeologists do. Yet we persist in training predominantly academic archaeologists."

The issue is not how archaeologists can make those people who love Heinrich Schliemann, Indiana Jones, Lara Croft and *Time Team* more interested in their own version of archaeology. The issue is rather what these popular figures can tell the professionals about popular themes and interests they need to address themselves (cf. Moore 2006). As a major report of the Economic and Social Research Council in the U.K. recently stated, the problem is not one of a lack of "public understanding of science" but increasingly it is one of a lack of scientific understanding of the public (Hargreaves and Ferguson 2000).

Approaching the field

The project discussed in this book continues my research into the interrelations between archaeology and popular culture (Holtorf 2004, 2005). The plan was to compare the portrayal of archaeology in the popular culture of three European countries: Germany, where I grew up, became fascinated by archaeology and began studying it; Great Britain, where I lived for many years first during my studies and then as an academic teacher and researcher; and finally Sweden, where I intended to work on this project, within the professional environment of the National Heritage Board. This choice of countries was determined more by various practical considerations than by the topic of my research in its own terms. To some extent I needed to take into account the United States as well, since

so much of European popular culture derives from there. During my research it became increasingly clear, however, that the differences of the image of archaeology among these countries are not very large. Thanks to Hollywood and the global economy, most popular characterisations apply more or less equally throughout the Western World. This is why this book does not contain any systematic analysis of existing differences between the countries I have been mostly looking at. However, outside Europe and the Western world, the entire picture is likely to be very different (cf. Shepherd 2002), but this will be for others to investigate and discuss in the future.

- "Professor, you stand accused of elitism and a disregard of popular community interests. How do you plead?"

I did not work with any rigid definition of popular culture (in German I prefer the term *Alltagskultur* – cf. Holtorf 2005: chapter 1). I am simply considering the main opportunities where people who are not archaeologists themselves and go about their ordinary lives can hear or see something that strikes them as being "archaeological". That includes the mass media, movies, advertising, toys, fictional and non-fictional literature, museums and much more. I found a broadly ethnographic methodology best suited for my ambition to shed light on how archaeology is presented in all that popular culture. The empirical research I conducted involved me visiting places, talking to people, watching films, reading books and studying all kinds of other available documents and material culture. The latter is significant for in a way my research can also be seen as a contribution to (historical) archaeology's tradition of studying everyday life by treating popular culture as neither innocent nor trivial (Little 1991).

Although it is clear that the "general public" has got to be broken down into many specific audiences, I am not seeking to make too many fine-grained distinctions as to precisely which sections of the populations may be interested in what aspect of archaeology. This book is, however, *not* about how professional archaeologists themselves see their own subject (see Welinder 2000).

Popular culture is diverse and many of its lines follow their own logic and their own genealogies. At the same, elements of popular culture have in common that fairly large numbers of people can relate to them and appreciate what they are about. At one point I thought it might be a good idea to draw on social psychology for understanding precisely why people may find archaeology appealing in the way they do. I could not find any detailed research by social psychologists that offered answers to my specific question but I read Serge Moscovici's (1984) grand proposal for studying "social representations." Much of it seemed to be applicable to my own study, too. I also read some of the arguments of his critics though and in the end I did not feel that all this was leading anywhere very useful for the purposes of this book. More applicable was the topical secondary literature that archaeologists have published over the years.

A particular long tradition of discussing the popular fascination with archaeology exists in Germany (e.g. Kirchner 1964; Steuben 1977; Andreae 1981; Stern and Tode 2002; Felder et al 2003). In Sweden, the available literature is smaller but what exists is no less inspiring (e.g. Welinder 1987; Petersson 1994). In the United Kingdom, this field appears to be less discussed than many other realms of archaeology but some important work has been carried out here too (e.g. Daniel 1964: chapter 8; Bray 1981; Day 1997; Russell 2002a: Hall 2004). Additional literature that I found useful comes from various other countries (e.g. Ascher 1960; Pallottino 1968; Fritz 1973; Zarmati 1995; Cohodas 2003; Hendriks 2005). The content of all these studies is too diverse for me to summarise it here, even if in abbreviated form. In subsequent chapters I will return to many of the specific issues these works raise.

***

I wrote this book less as a single, coherent argument and more as a series of interrelated essays, dealing in turn with particularly important aspects of my subject. In this introduction I introduced my project and outlined some broader trends and developments in both society and archaeology. Chapter 2 takes the form of a travel log from one of my fact-

finding missions, in this case to the U.K. It demonstrates the variety and omnipresence of archaeology in daily life and popular culture. Of particular significance to Western popular culture are the mass media, especially television and newspapers and these I will turn to in Chapter 3. There are both general trends in the way the media portray archaeology as well as a few peculiarities for each of the three countries I have been looking at in detail. However, what the media show may not be the same as what their audiences actually know and like about archaeology. Chapter 4 is therefore discussing the (relatively few) existing opinions polls and surveys of people's perceptions of archaeology and archaeologists. Chapter 5 reviews a wide range of popular culture representations, including movies, fiction and non-fiction literature. Four key themes of what archaeology is about are introduced and discussed. What are professional archaeologists to make of these themes and associated stereotypes? In chapter 6, I will discuss the main strategies available to archaeologists in engaging with their popular representations. Finally, chapter 7 is going to present a summary of the previous argument and an outlook for future practice. I will be concluding that a socially relevant archaeology needs to take (more) seriously where the popular demand and the appeal of archaeology actually lie. For archaeology may be an academic discipline but even more so it is a widely recognized, positively valued and well underpinned brand.

Chapter 2

A travel log

Sunday, 11 May 2003

I arrive at Stansted Airport from Stockholm. My fact-finding mission to the United Kingdom has begun. Just how many references to archaeology will I come across in popular culture as I travel for the next six days through England? It doesn't start well: the airport features a promising shop of the 'Past Times' chain but although the past is ubiquitous here I see no explicit reference to archaeology, however long I walk around in this shop full of nostalgic merchandise.[7]

On the train to Peterborough things improve. I read the 'Independent-on-Sunday' and quickly come across an ad for PlayStation games including 'Indiana Jones and the Emperor's Tomb' ("Buy 2 get 3rd free"). I also note in the TV programme that 'Indiana Jones – Raiders of the Lost Ark' will be shown on BBC 1 at 6pm this very evening. It is self evident that my mission will require me to watch this film (once more).

I pick up the 'Great North Eastern Railways' train magazine as well as some tourist brochures and am duly reminded to visit Flag Fen, "a significant European archaeological site", which – thanks to the work of a dedicated team of archaeologists – provides "fascinating insight into early civilization." One of the brochures promises that at the same site I will be able to "enjoy a unique archaeological experience" and I may even be able to observe "archaeologists at work". Clearly, this archaeological experience needs to be visited. Fortunately, I have already arranged for a meeting with the Project Director tomorrow morning.

Before I withdraw to my Bed & Breakfast accommodation (and the promised archaeological movie) I take an afternoon stroll through the busy shopping town of Peterborough. I come passed the Museum & Art Gallery which is closed. A display board gives a glimpse of what they are offering otherwise: From 'Vikings' and 'Rest In Peace: An exhibition about the rites, beliefs and practices of death in Peterborough,

---

[7] http://www.pasttimes.com

from the earliest times to the present day', to 'Egyptians: Travel back to the mysterious world of Ancient Egypt!' and the 'Peterborough Ghost Walk'.

Elsewhere in town, I see another 'Past Times' shop, likewise without much archaeology in it, but in the section 'Distant Lands' there are at least some references to Ancient Egypt. Elsewhere I have more luck. In a 'Fine Art + Graphics Shop' there are three framed posters of characters in the TV series 'Stargate SG-1' which was introduced after the success of the archaeological movie 'Stargate' (1994). I noted later that the series is also currently shown on the British TV station Sky One, Wednesdays at 6pm (three hours after 'Relic Hunter').

That same fine art shop is also selling cards with famous cinematic motifs, among them Chimpanzee archaeologist Dr Cornelius and his wife Dr Zira in front of three crucified apes (from the 1967 version of 'The Planet of the Apes', with a story about forbidden archaeological knowledge...). In the same shop I also spot a signed poster of Harrison Ford as 'Indiana Jones'. It sells – or rather has not yet sold – for £175. Is this the going rate for something touched by the greatest popular archaeologists of them all I wonder, while watching him a little later, from the comfort of my bed, "at work".

Later that evening I decide to go to a movie. The 'Showcase Cinema' welcomes me with a big cardboard poster announcing yet another famous movie archaeologist: "Coming Soon ... Lara Croft. Tomb Raider. The Cradle of Life". But she is not here yet, so I decide to watch the film 'Bulletproof Monk' instead. It turns out to be a martial arts movie about a Tibetan monk trying to protect an ancient scroll, holding the power to dominate the universe, from some Nazi-like enemies. Sounds pretty much like an Indiana Jones script, but nobody in the film is in fact (meant to be) an archaeologist.

Monday, 12 May 2003

I get up early. On the way to Flag Fen, I walk past a discount bookstore where I soon spot videos on sale. Among them is 'Star Trek Deep Space 9, vol 4', containing the episode "q-less" featuring sexy Vash, a female archaeologist and former love-interest of Captain

Picard. She is engaged in tomb-robbing and the illicit antiquities trade and has been known to dress in beautiful colonial style fashion. I happily pay £1 for the video and make my way to that significant European archaeological site a short distance out of town.

There is no real footpath so I end up having to cross a muddy ploughed field. Suddenly I note a strangely shaped flint lying in front of me. It's a broken prehistoric tool but it may take an archaeologist to recognise it as such. Although strictly speaking this field may not be part of popular culture, both expertise and finder's luck are available to all in society too.

At Flag Fen[8] I meet Francis Pryor, discoverer of the site and long-time director of its excavations, currently also President of the 'Council for British Archaeology' (CBA). Besides all that, he is a successful archaeological author and TV presenter (e.g. 'Britain BC', BBC 2003). Pryor arrives in a battered Land Rover, with a trowel on the seat next to him. The perfect entry for a field archaeologist.

We have a long chat in one of the reconstructed roundhouses at Flag Fen and finally end up in a pub in Peterborough, still talking. Among other things, Pryor tells me that the sand-pit on the site allows children by themselves to find things (that had earlier been planted). That notion of discovery is one children love, whether at Flag Fen or in TV programmes like 'Time Team'. It's the thrill of doing archaeology! The British success series 'Time Team' has of course also filmed at Flag Fen and that in itself has become a part of the history of the site. A display features various images from the filming and a poster signed by the 'Time Team' heroes themselves.

In the afternoon I take the train and travel on to York. I buy a copy of the 'Daily Express' at the station but find no archaeology mentioned anywhere.

I arrive at York train station on a very pleasant early summer afternoon. The first thing I notice is a huge advertising poster announcing "JORVIK. THE AUTHENTIC VIKING ENCOUNTER" and similar messages are contained in all of the available tourist brochures. After all, 'Jorvik' and the attractions of the 'York Archaeological Trust' (YAT) are among the biggest crowd-pullers for the city of York. During my stay I will meet both Peter Addyman, who set the YAT up some thirty years ago and John Walker, the present Chief Executive.

---

[8] http://www.flagfen.com

Still at the train station, I notice that the tourist office there offers a leaflet entitled 'Time Team in York'. I am intrigued and hand over the 50p it costs. Such has been the influence of 'Time Team' on the popular consciousness in the United Kingdom that visitors choose to visit York in the footsteps of the TV show that in September 1999 excavated three sites in the centre of the town. The following year, visitor numbers at 'Jorvik' were up by 100,000.

By the same token, what present "do you get the person who has got everything?" The YAT charges £50 for "A Day on the Dig", during which you "will be following in the footsteps of television's 'Time Team', discovering the latest about our ancestors…".[9]

After checking into my Bed and Breakfast accommodation, I go for a stroll through town. 'The Haunted Walk of York' is advertised for the same evening and I decide to take part. Tony is our guide and he tells us ghost stories as well as gory histories while walking through York's old town centre. These are stories his grandmother told him as a child, stories he heard from other York citizens and accounts of what happened to members of groups like ours in the past… His account includes

- ghosts in the King's Manor which now houses the University's Department of Archaeology;

- a Viking ghost living in St. Saviour's Church, now YAT's 'Archaeological Resource Centre' (more on that below);

- YAT excavations at the Treasurer's House confirming the existence of a Roman Road, precisely where previously Roman soldiers had been witnessed walking half submerged on the level of their own road;

- excavations in 1964 at the Tax Office Building which confirmed a legend about particularly gory killings of Christians by Vikings.

Whereas the first two examples contribute to creating a certain spooky ambience for modern archaeology, the latter two employ archaeological excavations as evidence for the trustworthiness of paranormal experiences and folk legends.

---

[9] Now available at http://web.archive.org/web/20030417032541/http://www.yorkarchaeology.co.uk/present.htm

Tuesday, 13 May 2003

In the morning I walk once more through the historic town centre of York, on the search for an Internet Cafe from where to check my email. The entire town centre has a distinctly historical feel to it. One shop is called 'Past Images' and it offers to take your family picture, with everybody wearing Viking clothes and a stereotypical long boat in the background.

At lunch time I meet up with Mike Heyworth, Deputy Director and Jonathan Bateman, Information Officer, of the 'Council for British Archaeology' (CBA).[10] The are CBA promotes archaeology in the UK, involving consultancy work for the media and the production of a popular magazine 'British Archaeology'. The current issue has an ad on the back inviting students to "Explore the past… by distance learning" at the University of Leicester. The CBA also runs the 'Young Archaeologists' Club', with 67 branches in the U.K., where all children are welcome to develop their interest in archaeology: "Get the worm's eye view"!

Through a special working party, the CBA also sponsors the biannual 'Channel 4 Award' for the best archaeological film or video. Among past winners was Channel 4's own series 'Time Team'.

It is often especially through comedy that the nature and impact of a phenomenon in popular culture becomes evident. Bateman points me to a recent BBC parody of the currently en vogue TV genre of history and archaeology documentaries. The comedian Marcus Brigstocke wrote 12 short episodes of a series entitled 'We are History', in which he plays the authoritative historian David Oxley, B.A. (Hons). I borrow the tape and later laugh out loud about the hilarious way in which Brigstocke makes fun of TV historian Simon Schama, the BBC docu-soap 'Surviving the Iron Age', Julian Richards series 'Meet the Ancestors' and 'Time Team's' Tony Robinson, among others.

Alex Hunt, then the CBA's Research and Conservation Officer, writes press statements on behalf of the CBA and tells me of the difficulty to give stories the right "spin" in order to make them interesting for journalists. In other words, for archaeological stories to acquire wider relevance they have to be billed as something other than what archaeologists think they are about. It means that few people are interested in archaeology in the same way archaeologists are interested in it. The CBA's own 'British Archaeology' magazine,

---

[10] http://www.britarch.ac.uk

too, reveals its ambition to reach wider audiences than its own membership when it titles in large letters: "Hunting for the first humans in Britain... Nick Ashton reports on our first half million years", or "Supernatural power dressing ... materials like jet, amber, faience and tin were also worn as talismans, writes Alison Sheridan." I ask myself: are archaeologists trying to sell to others their own interest in archaeology and the past – or have others already sold the popular interest in archaeology and the past to the archaeologists?

- "Seminal work my dear fellow, your arguments and findings challenge current discourse ..... but you are going to have to sex-up the title!"

Later that day, I watch a BBC 2 documentary on Michael Ventris, who in 1952 deciphered Linear B, Europe's earliest known writing system. The programme, entitled 'A Very English Genius', portrays Ventris as a mysterious amateur genius who suffered a mysterious death at 34, only four years after being able to proclaim that the mystery of Linear B had been solved. Although strictly speaking not about an archaeologist, the programme tells an archaeological story about a genius, a death and many associated mysteries, only some of which have been resolved.

Wednesday, 14 May 2003

The university town of York does of course have a comic shop which also sells postcards of famous film posters. Among them are posters for 'Lara Croft Tomb Raider' (2001) and

for all three 'Indiana Jones' films. The slogan that went with 'Raiders of the Lost Ark' (1981) sums up nicely how a film archaeologist could gain such popularity: Indiana Jones embodies "The Return of the Great Adventure" (see chapter 5).

My own adventures bring me next to the 'National Trust Shop'. They sell a children non-fiction book on "The Savage Stone Age", as part of the 'Horrible Histories' series which covers "history with the nasty bits left in".[11] The booklet contains a section on the history of archaeology, entitled "awful archaeologists". There I come across a very moving story about the (fictitious) Austrian archaeologist Gerhardt Katz who in 1957 committed suicide because the advent of radiocarbon dating had proved his own theories wrong. What is it with this dating method that threatens peoples' confidence in themselves (see also Mitchell 1977)? Hmh.

Then it's time for the Borders bookshop. Among many strictly academic titles, which are not my concern here, I come across 'The Complete Idiot's Guide to Lost Civilizations' (Ryan 1999). The front and back covers make it plain that this book was written for a large audience (at least as large as that of the 'Horrible Histories' books!). Its author is introduced as "Don Ryan, Ph.D., scholar and explorer" whose "many discoveries include the finding of lost tombs and controversial mummies." The reader of this "inside introduction to the exciting world of archaeology" is promised "the latest discoveries of mummies and tombs", "the facts on mythical worlds, such as Atlantis and Troy" and learn not only about "detailed explanations

- "..... and now to introduce our next act.....
THE ARCHAEOLOGISTS
you all know them from the blockbuster films....
....hold on to your sides and your hats
as they take you on a fun,
exciting, sexy, dangerous and adventurous
ride into the past"

[11] http://www.scholastic.co.uk/zone/book_horr-histories.htm; see also http://www.horrible-histories.co.uk

of the pyramids and the Mayan ruins" but also about "the dirt on artefacts and dating techniques." Confidently and in large letters, the publishers tell us that, fortunately, "you don't have to be Indiana Jones to learn about lost civilizations!" Evidently they have carefully considered what a lay person could possibly want from an introduction to archaeology.

What bothers me more than explicit populism is a certain ambiguity that becomes obvious in books like this. On the one hand, archaeology is portrayed as "an exciting field of study, full of mystery and adventure – a field where tiny bits of stone and bone can reveal great stories and where lost temples can still be found in the jungle" – from Ryan's address to the reader on the inside cover. But then, instead of explicitly celebrating the excitement, mystery and adventure of archaeology, instead of simply telling the great stories about past lives and present discoveries, the reader gets sobered up on the first page of the first chapter: "Superficially, archaeology might look like just a lot of fun and adventure, but it's actually a very sophisticated and scientific field of study" (Ryan 1999: 4). A little later Indiana Jones is debunked too:

> "Sorry to break the news, but as fun as it is to watch the dashing professor being chased by evil thugs, archaeology is usually not quite like this. ... The average archaeologist spends infinitely more time in the laboratory measuring potsherds and arrowheads than avoiding volleys of poison arrows in the Amazon or narrowly escaping ancient booby traps."

Jones is subsequently outed as "a fake", but Ryan and his fellow archaeologists are said to be "real", as are their discoveries. That, we are told, "makes true archaeology all the more fascinating" (1999: 6). I am not sure though if the rest of the book can really live up to this standard.

I argued in 'From Stonehenge to Las Vegas' (Holtorf 2005) that the value and significance of archaeology is largely rooted in the "archaeo-appeal" it conveys and not in the extent to which a time-traveller would actually recognize the past in our reconstructions of it. As archaeologists we ought to be celebrating that appeal, openly and unashamedly. That is why, in the end, Ryan has it right after all, when he admits that "archaeology is one of those professions that seems almost too good to be true" ...

"sort of like being a ski instructor all year round" (p. 309, 311).

I am almost late for my lunch appointment with Peter Addyman who, in 1972, founded a charity with the name 'York Archaeological Trust' (YAT).[12] The popularity of its visitor attraction 'Jorvik', formerly The 'Jorvik Viking Centre', is almost too good to be true, too. Since it opened in 1984, nearly 14 million paying visitors have been on a spectacular ride through the reconstructed Viking age settlement of 'Jorvik', boosting York's tourist economy by £25 million every year. At one point, the number of school parties had to be restricted to one every 13 minutes. The numerous visitors effectively subsidise extensive academic research programmes of the YAT in perpetuity. Fittingly, the 'Jorvik' experience contains a reconstructed excavation site where you can see models of YAT employees you have sponsored "at work", practicing what Addyman describes as the "fantastic science" of archaeology.

For Addyman, scientific integrity and credibility are everything. All the various attractions run by the YAT were therefore designed to be accurate to the highest academic standards. At the same time, this authenticity is packaged and promoted to the public by using the latest communication and marketing techniques. Although Addyman, the archaeologist, admits to having at home a set of Indy's hat and whip as used in 'Raiders of the Lost Ark', misleading stereotypes in the manner of Indiana Jones and Lara Croft were to be carefully avoided in his attractions. Despite this qualification, satisfying visitor expectations has been considered paramount at 'Jorvik'. Addyman realised that only if the product on offer was perceived as entertaining, enjoyable and worthwhile would many people be coming and be willing to pay a reasonable amount for it. That is the reason why 'Jorvik' is never called a "museum" but is instead billed as an experience and "Viking encounter".

"You learn more when it is not a museum," says the founding director of what must be one of the most successful archaeological enterprises in the world. The educational messages 'Jorvik' contains – about the Viking age, archaeological practice and the need to protect or rescue archaeological sites – are partly conveyed on a subliminal level rather than through explicit didactics. Addyman's admits to having been inspired a lot by Vance Packard's 'The Hidden Persuaders' (1960), a study of how advertisers employ depth psychology to influence people's choices in daily life.

---

[12] http://www.yorkarchaeology.co.uk

Ever since he began charging people a fee for observing the on-going YAT excavations in the centre of York and sold them souvenirs, Peter Addyman's strategy has been to give the people (some of) what the people want, while letting them subsidise an ambitious programme of urban archaeology in return. Simultaneously he supplied his paying visitors with subliminal messages that were, in his judgment, good for them and good for archaeology. As a result, 'Jorvik' manages to attract many of those who would never normally visit a museum, subsequently letting "a monster" "brainwash" them with archaeological "propaganda" – all words he has used.

In a lecture given a few years ago, which Addyman showed me, he summarised his approach by stating that

> "the Jorvik Viking Centre is a purpose-designed educating machine, developed on principles of efficiency and cost-effectiveness; predicated on academic integrity, education values and the belief that learning can … be fun; and using advanced modern techniques of presentation, persuasion, delivery and marketing."

Seldom have I come across such a cool, measured and smart approach, exploiting the public fascination with archaeology for 'higher' aims than merely making money.

In the afternoon I go to see the refurbished 'Jorvik' for myself, at £7.20 not cheap but at least I am supporting a charity. The ride is impressive, no doubt about it. What is more, everything in the reconstructed Viking city is claimed to be based on the "painstaking excavation work of York Archaeological Trust" so that, at one point, "..you are looking directly in a face of a resident of Viking Age Jorvik". Archaeology becomes a "fantastic science" indeed, too good to be true.

Thursday, 15 May 2003

I have an appointment with John Walker who not long ago succeeded Peter Addyman at the top of the YAT. I want to get his view of popular archaeology and the approach the Trust is taking now.

On the way to his office I pass an antiquities shop, 'Ancient Worlds', where

archaeological discoveries are offered for sale to collectors and visitors. Archaeology recovering commodities. A bit further on are the premises of the astrologer: 'Jonathan Cainer Horoscopes'. The stock in his shop, filled with New Age sounds and a scent of incense, includes books about 'The Maya and Sacred Stones' as well as many things Egyptian, including a miniature pyramid. Archaeology providing spiritual experiences.

John Walker is an interesting chap with interesting views. He reckons that archaeology only exists because people think it should exist. Walker argues therefore that the YAT needs to refocus on the fundamental question of public benefit and reconsider how to use the widespread image of archaeology to appeal to wider audiences. He believes that in principle "archaeology is a passport to every class", allowing access to all groups in society. YAT's current Chief Executive is thus quite willing to incorporate Lara Croft and Indiana Jones in the promotion of archaeology at York. A few weeks after my visit, YAT released a press statement entitled 'Become 'Indiana Jones' this summer at the JORVIK Explorers Club', offering children the chance to "travel through time, handle ancient objects, learn the tools of the archaeology trade and even meet people from the past!"[13]

Walker is not at all certain why so many people actually visit the 'Jorvik' exhibit – although numbers have been declining. Of course the popular fascination with the Vikings plays a role, as does the perfect location in the centre of York. Walker also wonders precisely what Jorvik achieves in educational terms. It is clear to him that visitors love the sensation of discovering something amazing, whether that is of material value or a new insight. Maybe that feeling of finding a treasure, once enjoyed by Schliemann and Carter, is also what makes modern tourists want to take a ride through a Viking age town?

For Walker, archaeology is essentially about exploration. He explains that archaeologists are space travellers moving backwards in time, exploring foreign worlds. In a way, therefore, archaeologists study "the Vikings as aliens", as Walker puts it. Consequently, the new slogan which he proposes for YAT is "to explore and explain."

John Walker then walks me to YAT's special educational facility, the 'Archaeological Resource Centre' (ARC), whose slogan draws on a different metaphor: "Become an

[13] http://www.jorvik-viking-centre.co.uk/getinvolved/archive.htm

archaeological detective..." (see chapter 5). He introduces me to Ian Carlisle and his deputy Tom Gibson who run the ARC which is mainly designed for school groups but promises "great fun for all age groups and abilities". I learn that all children who visit are familiar with 'Time Team'. Here they are being introduced to the post-excavation work that receives somewhat less attention in the TV series. All children are allowed and indeed expected to handle real artefacts ("you are here to work!"). Quickly, they get immersed in their very own little lab work. Gibson says that sometimes he wears a white coat to heighten the scientific experience. Children love that, as they love playing being on 'Time Team' and handling charismatic artefacts such as animal skulls and the Viking Age pooh found below Lloyds Bank. The appeal is clear. As the leaflet promises, at ARC you can "hold history in your hand."

The ARC presents a scientistic archaeology. It's all bones and pot shards and samples and microscopes and hypotheses. And white coats (sometimes). And popular among children it is, too.

Later that evening I read two local papers, 'The Evening Press' and 'The Northern Echo'. The only reference to archaeology I come across is a featured walk passing by a Roman fort, a small section of which has been excavated. In this case, archaeology supplies ramblers with destinations in the landscape. Here as elsewhere, what is hinted at and evoked by ancient remains – untouched by archaeological detectives – can encourage contemplations about past people and the course of history (see also Burström 2004).

Friday, 16 May 2003

I am on my way home! In the train from York I find a 'Daily Mirror'. The only references to archaeology are in the TV programme and among the events listings where all heritage attractions appear in a category called "Adventure." A larger feature is dedicated to artefacts from the 'Titanic' on display at the Science Museum in London. A recovered porthole from the ship provides the visual anchor for a short story about "A window on history."

During a stopover back in Peterborough, I notice in a major shopping centre a stand of the local council advertising its own heritage attractions. Among them is, of course, Francis Pryor's Flag Fen where visitors can "discover the world of the ancestors."

Later, I pick-up a leaflet for a performance of Händel's opera 'Serse' (Xerxes) in Cambridge. Prominently displayed is a fragmented stone relief of Xerxes. I wonder about the significance of archaeology as a supplier of evocative images that can crop up pretty much everywhere...

My last few hours in the UK. Looking back. It's been an intensive week. I encountered popular archaeology in pretty much all plausible and some implausible places. I came across a wide range of different appeals of archaeology and a similar wide range of different strategies using these appeals. That currency of archaeology and the amazing variety of its uses in popular culture has been the main result of my trip and that is also the main message of this chapter. The next chapter will look in some depth at the meaning of archaeology in the mass media.

Chapter 3

Archaeology in the mass media

In this chapter I will look at the meaning of archaeology in TV and newspapers in the United Kingdom, Sweden and Germany and discuss both emerging differences between them and general trends they share.

TV stations and newspapers are playing a particularly important role in contemporary popular culture. According to research published online by the British TV station *Channel 4*, British adults watch every day an average of about four hours TV (Americans reportedly watch more) and only 0.6% of the adult population state that they "never watch commercial TV". What is more, 15-24 year olds consider "watching TV" and "reading newspapers" as the most important social activities to make time for (45% and 41% agreement respectively).[14] To a greater extend than any other media TV programmes and newspapers are both influencing and reflecting what people know and how they think.

I am assuming here that TV programmes and newspaper articles are significant indicators for larger trends in popular culture. From a methodological standpoint, it is important to realise though that the reason for that is not that producers and editors simply decide what very large audiences, for lack of choice, get to watch or read. As far as the largest part of their revenues is concerned, contemporary mass media are not in the business of distributing content to paying audiences. Instead, they are selling audiences to advertisers. What is shown on TV or printed in newspapers can be seen as a means of reaching particular sections of the population that certain companies consider profitable to reach with their ads. It is therefore essential for TV stations and newspaper editors to know and address the interests of these audiences and a large amount of market research is dedicated to learning about them through usually confidential research. The fact that particular stations and papers continue, or come, to exist is an indication that they succeed in this aim better than their competitors with alternative content. The methodological risk of media analyses is thus less that one extrapolates from the personal preferences of the few individuals ultimately responsible for their content, but that they will focus too much on the existing preferences of those sections of the population which are most attractive for advertisers – often 16-54 year olds with good incomes.

---

[14] http://www.channel4sales.com

The situation is slightly different regarding state-regulated media such as public service TV stations (e.g. SVT in Sweden, ZDF and ARD in Germany, the BBC in the U.K.). Instead of simply selling advertising space, they are receiving license fees from all TV viewers but are in exchange subjected to complicated, politically motivated regulations. It is therefore harder to infer about popular culture from public service TV. In practice, however, these channels – in order to justify their privileges – compete increasingly (though less exclusively) for the same audiences as commercial channels. Their content thus often expresses the same trends.

Archaeology on TV

Among businesses it is well known that television advertising is still the best way to get messages across to wide sections of the population. The sciences have long realised the power of the medium of TV, too. As long ago (in media terms) as 1987, the American George Gerbner (1987: 115), a Professor of Communications, pointed out that a single episode on prime-time television reaches more people than all science and technology promotional efforts put together. More importantly, he argued that television reaches those who receive no other information about science. This is probably also true for archaeology. We know that TV is the population's single most important source of information about archaeology (cf. chapter 4). Besides archaeological movies and documentaries, even news and children's programmes as well as animated series can contain references to archaeology that contribute to the overall picture TV viewers, i.e. nearly the entire population, form in their minds of archaeology.

In 2001/2, two adventures of the film archaeologist Indiana Jones were each watched by an audience of more than 10 million British people, resulting in rankings among the top ten programmes shown on BBC 1 during that year. In addition, in 2001 alone, the five terrestrial British TV channels taken together broadcast 31 series and 19 single documentaries with archaeological content (see box below). According to another study, between 1998 and 2002, 651 archaeological documentary programmes (including repeats and episodes within series) were scheduled on the four British channels BBC 1, BBC 2, Channel 4 and ITV. The most popular ones attracted more than 5 million viewers (Kulik 2003b). Probably even higher figures could be cited for some historical documentaries.

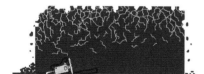

Archaeology in *The Simpsons*[15]

In the classroom, Skinner makes an announcement over the intercom

- *Attention, all honour students will be rewarded with a trip to an archaeological dig.* [The honour students cheer].

- *Conversely, all detention students will be punished with a trip to an archaeological dig.* [The detention students boo].

Soon enough, the field trip is underway. Jimbo, Dolph and Kearney are pick-axing into the ground, wearing prisoner-style outfits.

Lisa: *This is so exciting, I can't wait to see what we to find.*

Skinner: *I must admit, this is rather exciting. Eh! Look there's something right here. It seems to be some sort of rock!* [picks it up and crumbles it] *Oh no, it is just a clump of dirt. Even so, my heart is pounding like a kettle drum, I better sit down for a while.* [sits and wipes brow].

Elsewhere on the site, Ralph seems to have found something!

Ralph: *Principal Skipple, Principal Skimpster. I found something.* [all gather]
It's a spearhead.

Miss Hoover: *That's your trowel blade, Ralph, it fell off the handle.*

Ralph: *And I found it.*

In this light it is hardly surprising that in 2001 the First World Congress of History TV Producers celebrated historical documentaries as "the new rock'n'roll", being one of the few thriving sectors of the media (Willis 2001). The film historian Karol Kulik (2003a) argued accordingly that the period roughly from 1995 to 2001 should be considered a "golden age" of archaeology in the British mass media (an earlier "golden age" had occurred during the 1950s and 60s – cf. Jordan 1981, Schadla-Hall and Morris 2003).

Unlike businesses, archaeological institutions like state heritage authorities, universities and museums have not conducted very much research in order to find out precisely who is watching which kind of archaeological programme, what TV audiences associate with archaeology and which messages they are actually getting out of programmes with archaeological content. Many archaeologists still think that the most important criterion for the way they are depicted in the mass media is the degree to which these representations conform to their own perception of being an archaeologist – "but *in reality* it's not as shown in that programme"; the extent to which the information conveyed

---

[15] abbreviated from http://www.snpp.com/episodes/5F05

would be academically defensible – "but you simply cannot put it *as simplistically as that*"; or whether it might harm their own professional interests in society – "but this implies that *anybody* could go and retrieve ancient artefacts" (see chapter 6). What is important to realise though is that the message of any TV programme is not only conveyed by what is literally said and shown but also by the overall impressions given in the film. For the most part, archaeologists are not very concerned with the overarching stories that are being told about the field of archaeology or any suggested associations. The Austrian archaeologist Elisabeth Pühringer (2000: 82) argued though that the most important messages of archaeological documentaries emerge "in between the images".

Archaeological documentary series on British terrestrial Television channels

Ancient Apocalypse	BBC 2	Meet the Ancestors	BBC 2
Ancient Secrets	BBC 2/	Mummies	Ch 4
	Ch 5	Mysteries of Lost Empires	Ch 4
Ancient/Great Civilizations	Ch 4	Raised from the Deep	Ch 4
The Battle of Hood and Bismarck	Ch 4	Search for Atlantis	Ch 5
Battleships	Ch 4	Secrets of the Ancients	BBC 2
Blood of the Vikings	BBC 2	Secrets of the Dead	Ch 4
Cannibal	Ch 4	Secrets of the Stone Age	Ch 4
Egypt's Golden Empire	BBC 2	Seven Wonders of the World	Ch 4
Empires of Stone	Ch 4	Son of God	BBC 1
The History of Britain from the Air	Ch 5	Surviving the Iron Age	BBC 1
Horizon	BBC 2	Talking Landscapes	BBC 2
House Detectives	BBC 2	The Celts	Ch 4
Invasion	BBC 2	Time Team	Ch 4
Journeys to the Bottom of the Sea	BBC 2	What the Romans Did for Us	BBC 2
Lost Gardens	Ch 4	What the Victorians Did for Us	BBC 2

Source: CBA 2001

Many of the programmes follow established models that attract predictable (fairly large) audiences. Famously, the British TV producer Bruce Norman (1983: 29) once suggested that "the best, i.e. most popular, [archaeological] programme would be the discovery of an Egyptian mummy with gold teeth on a submerged wreck off an island in the

Caribbean." Although this description of stereotypical archaeo-appeal may have been overstated to the extent that it was wrong even then (cf. Kulik 2003b), still today we can recognise certain popular clichés that reoccur in many archaeological documentaries. They are to do with exotic locations, adventurous fieldwork and spectacular discoveries. For example, a 1997 TV series entitled "Ice Mummies" contained one episode described in the following way[16]:

> "Frozen in Heaven. This is the bizarre and fascinating story of the remains of Inca culture, frozen for posterity high in the mountains of the Andes. Evidence has emerged of sacrifice to the mountain gods, whose existence dominated the civilization over 500 years ago. The film traces the frozen bodies of children uncovered by archaeologists in South America, and follows an archaeological expedition to a high-altitude sacred site in search of ritual remains and another body. How did they come to be there? Why did they go to their deaths willingly? What was the religious framework that dictated their sacrifice to fierce gods?"

No wonder, this series reached an absolutely astonishing figure of more than 5 million viewers in the UK alone (Kulik 2003b). It was also shown on PBS in the US and on Discovery Channel, indicating a similar appeal of that kind of archaeology across (at least) the Western world. But why is this appeal so similar in different countries? One reason might be that since the mid 1990s, a number of large American, commercial TV stations have emerged that are specialising in documentaries. Since archaeology is a very visual discipline, with exciting locations, various activities and evocative finds to film, among their documentaries are a fair number of archaeological programmes. The biggest channels now broadcast nearly

Global TV stations specializing in archaeological and other documentaries:

The History Channel
http://www.historychannel.com/, http://www.thehistorychannel.co.uk/

Discovery Channel
http://www.discovery.com/
http://www.discoveryeurope.com/

National Geographic Channel
http://www.nationalgeographic.com/channel/
http://www.ngceurope.com/

OLD POTS £1

---

[16] http://www.pbs.org/wgbh/nova/listseason/25.html#icemummies; see also http://www.pbs.org/wgbh/nova/icemummies

all over the entire world and the overwhelming similarity of popular perceptions about archaeology throughout the Western world is therefore hardly surprising. People are simply watching the same programmes.

Even so, there are a few observable regional peculiarities in the three countries I have been looking at in more detail: the U.K., Germany and Sweden. In each country, one specific series of programmes, representing a particular way of portraying archaeology, has been especially influential.

Germany: Gisela Graichen's adventure archaeology

Since the 1990s, public television archaeology in Germany has been influenced a great deal by the work of a single person and her collaborators: the writer Gisela Graichen. Her most significant TV series and subsequent book publications were *C 14 – Advances into the Past: Archaeological Discoveries in Germany* (several series, broadcast since 1992) and later *Schliemann's Heirs* (several series, broadcast since 1996).

C 14 was the first-ever dedicated TV series about archaeology in Germany. In each 30-minute episode, several short reports about different archaeological projects were presented. The featured sites were chosen in close co-operation with the various state archaeology services in Germany. At least two of the associated books also contained prefaces by Dieter Planck, then President of the Association of German State Archaeologists (Verband der Landesarchäologen). Possibly as a side-effect of the cooperation with official bodies, which is typical for the work of Graichen, the TV series was awarded the *German Prize for Heritage Preservation* (Deutscher Preis für Denkmalschutz).

The *C 14* series effectively married ordinary state archaeology and its high-tech methodologies with existing popular stereotypes of archaeology emphasising exciting quests for historical treasures and revelations by scientists about secrets of the past. Up to 1,7 million viewers turned on their television sets for each episode, corresponding to around 10% of the vital adult market (14-49 years old). Graichen demonstrated in this series that she understands that selling archaeological research works best by emphasising gold and treasures, even if this cliché needs to be modified somewhat now (see also Graichen 1995: 11). She explained once (Graichen 1999: 17, my translation) that "today, the adventure of archaeology consists not – only – in finding gold treasures. The treasure consists of the insights which high-tech methods can deliver about our past."

This approach was continued in *Schliemann's Heirs*, where already the title referred to the best-known stereotypical archaeologist in Germany. The name of Heinrich Schliemann evokes, still, a range of colourful associations about digs in foreign places, re-discovering lost empires, hidden golden treasures – and the eventual rewards of persisting with a controversial quest against much scholarly opposition and many practical obstacles. It was hardly surprising then that this series managed to attract regularly an even larger audience of around 5 million viewers or around 15% overall market share (again 10% of adult market). *Schliemann's Heirs* broadened out from archaeology in Germany and now embraced German projects carried out abroad. After all, Graichen (1993: 14, my translation) knows that "the search for the traces of the past is more likely to be touched by a sense of adventure when history is more distant from us – both in time and space." Again, the German film maker secured the support of the relevant state institution, in this case the *German Archaeological Institute* which is financed by the German Foreign Ministry.

The approach towards archaeology taken in all these films is well illustrated by some book and chapter titles of the accompanying publications: *Treasure hunters in Germany; Schliemann's heirs and the message of the* lost *cities; Angkor, the Atlantis in the jungle*. Graichen makes frequently explicit references to the Indiana Jones archaeological stereotype. For example, two chapter titles in one of the accompanying books (Graichen and Hillrichs 1999) refer to the German title of *Raiders of the Lost Ark* (*Jäger des verlorenen Schatzes*): *Der Jäger des vergrabenen Schatzes* and *Das Tal des verlorenen Baches*.

Graichen's TV programmes and associated book publications have grown out of a tradition of depicting the life and work of scientist/adventurers on their explorations. That tradition is not restricted to Germany but it has been particularly popular there, even over recent decades (Stern 2002). Immediately after World War II, C. W. Ceram (1980) wrote his "fact-based archaeological novel" in this broad genre, as did later followers such as Philipp Vandenberg and Rudolf Drößler. On the television screen, I remember watching throughout my childhood numerous episodes of a series entitled *Countries, Humans, Adventures* (*Länder, Menschen, Abenteuer*) about people in exotic places around the world, their cultures and ancient monuments and attempts by anthropologists,

OLD
POTS
£1

archaeologists and others to find out more about them. Amazingly, after more than 400 episodes since 1975, this series is still running. Since 1982, the rival public TV station (ZDF) in Germany produced a series called *Terra X*, adopting a similar general format. It likewise became very popular, attracting similar viewer numbers as *Schliemann's Heirs* and is still running. Various sorts of documentaries such as *Terra X* are currently shown under the label *ZDF Expedition*.[17] The ZDF homepage for archaeology can be found following along the online tree *Knowing & Discovering > History & Adventure > Archaeology*. The words used in all these titles are of course not coincidental but characteristic for what I will come to call (in chapter 5) "the A theme".

Archaeology on German TV, for example on Sunday 1 February 2004:

16:30	3sat	Schauplätze der Weltkulturen: Hue / Vietnam (Doku, 60')
17.15	SWR	Länder – Menschen – Abenteuer: Angkor Vat (Doku, 45')
19:00	BRalpha	Streifzüge durch das Mittelalter (5/5, 45'):
		Der Gigant auf dem Thron
19:30	ZDF	ZDF Expedition – Schliemanns Erben (Doku 4/4, 45'):
		Roms Limes im Orient
		64 v. Chr. erobern römische Truppen das heutige Syrien. Sie sicherten das eroberte Gebiet mit einem Schutzwall aus Wehrtürmen, Militärlagern und Kastellen. Wissenschaftler versuchen, seinen genauen Verlauf und die Schutztechniken zu rekonstruieren.
20:15	Phoenix	Terra X: Qumran (Doku, 45'): Die Schriftrollen vom Toten Meer
23:15	Phoenix	Rätsel der Vergangenheit (Doku 2/5, 45'):
		Die mittelalterliche Wurfmaschine

Source: Ernst Sontheim

Although German TV occasionally also broadcasts documentaries about archaeological rescue excavations within Germany itself, archaeology is still often portrayed within that mindscape of exotic place – exciting adventure – spectacular discovery. The image of the archaeologist in Germany is often a mixture of Schliemann, Carter and Indiana Jones – they are "exotic beings" carrying out exotic work (Schmidt 2000: 241; see also Stern and Tode 2002). When the first series of *C 14* was being broadcast even Graichen and her professional friends had been surprised about the large interest the archaeological site "Germany" attracted among wide sections of the population...

---

[17] http://zdfexpedition.zdf.de

Sweden: Göran Burenhult's exotic explorations

Göran Burenhult is an archaeologist at Gotland University College and author of the most important archaeological textbooks available in Swedish. He is also the best known professional archaeologist on Swedish TV. Between the mid 1980s and the early 1990s Burenhult produced a series of beautiful coffee-table books and TV documentaries about his research that combined archaeological fieldwork in Sweden with ethno-archaeological studies on various islands in the Pacific, especially Papua New Guinea and the Trobriand Islands. This took archaeology on Swedish TV into a completely new direction.

Previously archaeology had been seen as an affair for antiquarian scholars as well as for the King. Gustav VI Adolf (1882-1973) after all was an enthusiastic amateur archaeologist (Lagerqvist and Odelberg 1972). During the early 1980s a series of programmes on *The cradle of the Svea state* (*Svearikets Vagga*) by the journalist Dag Stålsjö, advocating a revisionist theory about the location of the historic town of Birka and the origin of the Swedish state, had caused much public attention. It culminated in a recorded panel discussion to which about a dozen archaeological and historical experts, virtually all males in suit and tie and some of them university professors, contributed with scholarly assessments of the questions at hand. The archaeologists representing the professional establishment came across as stuffy, conspiring against amateurs and biased towards Stockholm. Burenhult dealt with new issues in new ways and changed the image of archaeology in Sweden completely.

Göran Burenhults popular books with the publisher *Bra Böcker* and associated TV programmes on SVT:

1986. *Speglingar av det förflutna [Reflections of the past].* – Six 45 min TV episodes.

1989. *Kärlekens Öar. Möten med kula-folket på Trobriandöarna [Islands of Love. Meeting the kula-people on the Trobriand Islands].* – One 50 min TV episode.

1991. *I James Cooks kölvatten [In the wake of James Cook].* – Three 60 min TV episodes.

1992. *Stenmännen. Megalitbyggare och Människoätare [Stonemen. Megalithbuilders and maneaters].* – One 50 min TV episode

1993-1996 (ed.). *Bra Böckers encyklopedi om människans historia [Bra Böckers encyclopedia of human history].* Ten volume series covering the first humans, people of the Stone Age, Old World civilizations, New World and Pacific civilizations and traditional peoples today. Also available in English and German versions.

With his special interest in the inhabitants of paradise-like islands of the Pacific, Burenhult took the archaeology/exotic adventure connection further than most. He was also unusual as a TV author in being a prominent academic himself and reporting to a large extent about his own fieldwork. Yet as adventurous as his accounts were, Burenhult always maintained a strong subtext of positivistic science and frequently linked his exotic work back to Sweden. A good example is the first project he completed, a book and film series entitled "Reflections of the past" (1986). This project dealt with the lives of 'Stone Age people' in ancient Sweden and currently living on tropical islands of the Pacific. The book sold in excess of 130.000 copies and twice that many watched the TV series.

In both the book and the TV programmes, the explorer Burenhult comes across as a scientific expert who speaks authoritatively about the past. His research draws not only on new excavations on Gotland but also on satellite pictures, infra-red photography and geo-radar surveys. In addition, Burenhult's investigations involved Land Rover and helicopter rides as well as cruises on his yacht. He travelled to the homes of well-built former cannibals where the dark-skinned men use stone-axes and the women walk around bare-breasted. Wearing "colonial style" clothes in the film, he is the white explorer documenting what appears in the viewfinder of his photo and video cameras. Burenhult is interested in 'primitive' peoples' architecture and subsistence strategies as well as in their ceremonies and rituals. Having labelled this research as ethno-archaeology, his observations are continuously transferred back to archaeological sites in Sweden, thus bringing the Stone Age back to life as it were. By contributing in this way to our understanding of both contemporary and prehistoric peoples, Burenhult hopes to learn about human behaviour in general and to help humans in their future struggles for survival.

Parts of Burenhult's work certainly evokes some of the same themes and metaphors as the film stories and images we associate with Indiana Jones (see chapter 5). When I asked him how he felt about that link he accepted without hesitation that archaeological research is of course exciting and often leads to unexpected discoveries, thus sharing some of its wide appeal with how archaeology is portrayed in popular culture. At the same time Burenhult seemed genuinely surprised how anybody could confuse a film hero with actual reality and think that the Indiana Jones stereotypes were a reflection of how archaeologists are actually working. Arguably, it is less a question of getting confused about reality, though and more a question of the emergence of images and representations that simply merge fact and fiction.

Burenhult's work has been popular and his TV programmes, he said, have been sold to 15 different countries. But even in Sweden they did not reach viewing rates comparable to either Gisela Graichen's documentaries in Germany or *Time Team* in the UK. Recently, Burenhult featured again as a scientific expert on TV, discussing a series of archaeological documentaries about a murder case at Stonehenge, cannibalism among the American Anasazi and a lost Viking town on Gotland, broadcast within the context of Swedish state television's educational programmes.

In 2005, a brand-new archaeological series was launched on the Swedish state television station SVT. It reached phenomenal viewing rates of regularly more than 20% and occasionally over 30% market share. *Utgrävarna*, the excavators, features a team of professional archaeologists led by Jonna Ulin who are digging up the remains of 20th century sites throughout Sweden. Together with oral accounts and contemporary photographs, the artefacts discovered are employed as tools for evoking memories of ordinary Swedes. Unlike Burenhults exotic adventures, this latest turn of Swedish TV archaeology is about everybody's past back home. The archaeologists in the programme are less experts than facilitators of historic memories.

Great Britain: Time Team's digging detectives

The British archaeologist Warwick Bray (1981: 228) argued more than two decades ago that the stereotypical archaeologists in popular culture have remained unchanged since 1939 when "the clock stopped." Whether or not this was correct then, it is certainly no longer correct now (cf. Ascherson 2004). The TV documentary series *Time Team*, which Tim Taylor has been producing for Channel 4 since 1993, arguably revolutionised the portrayal of archaeology in the British media.[18] More than one hundred episodes have been filmed of this programme. According to data supplied by Channel 4, episodes broadcast in spring 2003 still attracted regularly around 3.4 million viewers and a very impressive 15-20% total market share (on average, 51% of the viewers were male and 56% were between 16 and 54 years old). These are astonishing figures, especially if you take into account that Channel 4's *Big Brother* series, now promising real sex on camera (broadcast after 10pm), attracted in May 2004 a very similar figure of 3.3 million viewers, or a 15% audience share!

---

[18] http://www.channel4.com/history/timeteam

The normal *Time Team* format is a one-hour programme documenting a three-day archaeological excavation at a chosen site in the U.K., but there have also been episodes filmed abroad and *Time Team Specials* with live reporting over the course of several days or showing what goes on "behind the scenes". The special characteristic of the *Time Team* format is that, on each site, a fairly down-to-earth, local historical question is being investigated by excavating in front of the cameras. The regular team featured in the series consists of presenter Tony Robinson (formerly seen as Baldrick in the comedy series *Blackadder*) and the professional archaeologists Mick Aston, Carenza Lewis and Phil Harding who have all become minor celebrities. In addition, there is a large team of support staff and a pool of experts that are consulted when evidence in their area of expertise comes to light. Besides excavations, the programmes also involve experiments and demonstrations with recreated techniques and reconstructed artefacts.

The British state archaeological service *English Heritage* has understood that this show provides a wonderful opportunity to improve its image and therefore made a point of involving some of its staff as regulars into the programme. In an internal newsletter *English Heritage's* Chief Archaeologist, David Miles, expressed the hope that they come across as "helpful and keen but representing standards and common-sense."

Two appreciations of *Time Team*:

"I have been watching and recording 'The Time Team' for several years now. It is fantastic! They have a problem they are trying to solve and they dig only if they have to. They go into great detail on why they do or do not do something. If you want to dispel the myth of the archaeologist as 'Indiana Jones', then the 'Time Team' is for you!"

(George Schneider, e-mail correspondence 2004)

"Time Team has all the elements of a good novel. It's a detective story, a thriller with twists and turns, and it nearly always has a sting in the tail. Yet the work of Time Team is more than 60 minutes of fun and frolics with a trowel: it's a thorough scientific exploration, bringing together the latest technology and local resources."

(Author unknown)[19]

[19] http://www.sciencenet.org.uk/articlesfeatures/archpal/timeteam.html

The enormous popularity of the series has a lot to do with two factors in particular. Firstly, *Time Team* thrives on the notion of archaeologists discovering a series of material clues gradually solving a hidden mystery, usually with the help of science. Secondly, *Time Team*'s appeal also relies on some very special personalities involved, particularly Tony Robinson who gets so reliably excited whenever new discoveries are made and has a very down-to-earth attitude, mediating between the viewers and the archaeological experts. On the extensive *Time Team* homepages hosted by Channel 4, Sally Beck explained likewise that "part of the success is down to presenter Tony Robinson, whose enthusiastic on-air explanations have been so successful in demystifying the process that the science of digging up the past has reached cult proportions." The archaeologists are colourful personalities and interesting to watch, too.

Although Ian Jacob, then head of the BBC, is reported to have stated in the late 1950s that the two most popular things on television are archaeology and show-jumping (Daniel 1964: 150), it is probably fair to say that during the 1990s *Time Team* has brought archaeology to the people in a way that had previously been unthinkable. On the programme's already mentioned webpages you can order not only the site reports and books associated with the series but also subscribe to the quarterly *Time Team* magazine *Trench One*. Through *Time Team*, archaeology has become a part of British everyday culture, said Peter Addyman when I met him in York (see chapter 2). In the past, local farmers may not have been all that interested in archaeology on their land and on-lookers of an excavation project may have asked questions like: "Have you found any gold yet?". Since the success of *Time Team*, Addyman explained, archaeologists are welcomed with the question "Will you do a geophys?" (That method has no doubt become a buzzword, most often pronounced "geofizz" as in the hilarious, home-produced video spoofs about the *Grime Team*[20] and in Marcus Brigstocke's parody series *We are History*).

I came across several archaeological sites in the UK advertising with the slogan "as seen on Time Team", so that the relations between archaeology and television appear to have come full circle: archaeology makes for attractive TV and TV now also makes for attractive archaeology. Likewise, besides its other achievements, *Time Team* has without doubt attracted many students to archaeology (Hills 2003: 209). By the same token, at Cambridge University the fame of the series also guarantees attractive academic teaching: Corpus Christi College mentions on its webpages among its teaching staff for Archaeology, "Carenza Lewis of Channel 4's 'Time Team'."

---

20 http://www.grimeteam.co.uk

Several decades ago, both Mortimer Wheeler (1890-1976) and Glyn Daniel (1914-1986) had also been popular archaeologists in their programme *Animal, Vegetable, Mineral?* and were even chosen as TV Personalities of the Year for 1954 and 1955 respectively. But their appeal was that of the intellectual and lovable professor who told stories about strange artefacts from long dead civilizations, not that of the digging archaeologist in the field around the corner (Jordan 1981; Russell 2002b: 43). *Time Team*, on the other hand, celebrates the dirt and the mud as well as the gradual process of learning about local history by investigating material clues. Compared with the stereotypical mummy with golden teeth on a Caribbean wreck, as proposed by Norman (see above), *Time Team* and other current British TV programmes tend to focus on an altogether different kind of archaeology: they present British sites, preferably of Roman or Anglo-Saxon age, associated with a human story about bodily remains of ancestors or how they lived (Kulik 2003b).

> **When can we expect to see the Time Team in the USA?**
>
> Answer: The thing I'd like to do, in the case of America is to say "Look, you are fascinated by pyramids, you are fascinated by "Holy Grails" and stuff like that. Well, there is another kind of archaeology which you find in the back gardens of American homes...amazing Indian artifacts, and that's the kind of archaeology the Time Team is really interested in... Washington's brewery, something like that, we're going to be there making that as exciting as all of that pyramid stuff, which, you know, what relevance does all that have to the average guy? We're into democratic archaeology, parish pump in America – we'll be in somebody's back garden in America in about a year's time, we hope."
>
> Bob Wishoff asked Tim Taylor, series producer of *Time Team*, in July 2003[21]

As stated in a press release accompanying the most recent *Time Team* book (Robinson and Aston 2002), "archaeology has never been so much fun. This book will inspire everyone to get out into their back gardens and start digging." That is precisely what was meant to happen during the single weekend of 28 and 29 June 2003, when *Time Team* invited everybody in the UK to take part in *The Big Dig*.[22] This project was intended to become "the biggest archaeological dig this country has ever seen". The idea was for people to find out

[21] http://www.dirtbrothers.org/timeteam/timtaylor.html
[22] http://www.channel4.com/history/microsites/B/bigdig

what may lie buried in their gardens by digging (and recording) test pits approximately 1 x 1 m large and up to 60cm deep. *Time Team* would broadcast the most promising projects in a series of special programmes, live on national television. This is a far cry from the programmes produced by Graichen and Burenhult in Germany and Sweden respectively, where the viewer is notoriously glued to the TV screen, marvelling at the adventures of others.

"Big Dig" you say? The wife thought you were installing one of those new water features that gardening bloke on the telly's always doing

Although professional guidance was offered both regionally and nationally, *the Big Dig* was nevertheless a very controversial undertaking. Whereas some professional archaeologists considered it a ludicrous project, more entertainment than research and also ethically wrong in its implications for the preservation of very many unthreatened sites, others warned against elitism and welcomed the chance for people to get involved in finding out about their own local history. In the end, approximately 1,400 archaeological test pits were dug as part of that campaign and the programmes were each watched by around two million British viewers, corresponding to an overall market share of circa 10%.

Recently, Channel 4 has launched a new archaeological series that combines the *Time Team* appeal and some of its staff, with a more dramatic narrative reminiscent of Indiana Jones scripts. *Extreme Archaeology* is drawing on archaeology's old affinity with adventure in unfamiliar locations. According to a pitch to advertisers, each programme shows:

"a race against time to rescue an important and often unique piece of evidence from the past and save it from destruction. Using state of the art geophysics and observation

43

equipment, a small group of multi-skilled archaeologists record and evaluate the site before it is destroyed. Their challenge – to get out of an area with the information intact. Whether climbing rock faces, hacking through jungle, diving or pot holing – nothing must stop them reaching their goal. The pressure is on as the battle against the elements pushes them to the limit of their abilities and teamwork becomes essential to their success. A challenge to save treasures against the clock..."[23]

As series director Mel Morpeth explains on the project webpages:

"We wanted to create a series that wouldn't be perceived as being just another archaeology TV show. Too often TV viewers see experts wading across muddy fields with paper maps being blown about by the wind. We wanted to bring archaeology bang up to date and into the 21st Century." [24]

if you ask me, archaeology doesn't get much more extreme than these theory books I have to read at university!

Intriguingly, one anonymous contributor to a recent discussion on an archaeological discussion group commented that the *Extreme Archaeology* website "looks like a university prospectus". Whether or not that is demonstrably true, the comment relates to the fact that university departments are increasingly competing with each other in attracting students to their degree programmes. The same appeal that makes or breaks archaeology on TV is also becoming increasingly important for the well-being of academic archaeology – at least in the U.K..

* * *

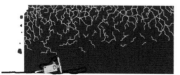

---

23   Now available at http://web.archive.org/web/20040618143341/http://www.televisioncorporation.co.uk/international/singleformats.php?pog=64
24   http://www.channel4.com/history/microsites/E/extremearchaeology/tech_gis.html

Each of these case-studies from the U.K., Sweden and Germany has to be understood within its specific cultural context and market. Nevertheless, they all share one thing, a common trend of portraying archaeology as a process rather than a set of results. Archaeology is about adventure and discovery, it involves explorations in exotic places (near or far) and it is carried out by digging detectives. Arguably, in popular culture, the research process – archaeologists in action – has actually become more important than the actual research results themselves (Rieche 1996: 154-5; Hills 2003: 208; Ascherson 2004: 156). Can this intriguing trend be confirmed from looking at the way archaeology is reported in newspapers?

Archaeology in Newspapers

Although TV programmes sometimes give a different impression, most archaeology is local archaeology. Indeed, according to Peter K. Betty (2002: 1056), publishing director with the British publisher *Tempus*, the wider interest in archaeology is generally stimulated by two main factors: television and local involvement. In terms of mass media, the interest in "all things local" is a domain of local and regional newspapers which have the space to report about a wide range of stories, often in considerable detail. An unpublished survey, which was conducted in 2003 by Ingrid Pfeiffer among 33 non-archaeologists of all ages, yielded the result that more than two thirds knew a local excavation site about which 17 (71%) had learned from newspaper reports and only 9 (38%) from TV reports. This indicates the significant role of newspapers. Although the influence of regional TV news is large too, people learn predominantly through newspaper reports about archaeological excavations that are going on in their own neighbourhood.

Archaeology in the press:

The CBA's British & Irish archaeology newsfeed:
http://www.britarch.ac.uk/newsfeed/index.html

Newsticker Archäologie (*Bild der Wissenschaft*) http://www.archaeologie-online.de/cgi-bin/links2/jump.cgi?ID=3397

Archaeologica News Update: http://www.archaeologica.org/NewsPage.htm

Just like archaeology has expanded over recent years on our TV schedules, newspapers too have become more interested in archaeological stories. In a survey of archaeological coverage in the British newspaper *The Daily Telegraph*, Karol

Kulik (2003a) could show that it had increased by over 700% (!) in one 18-month period during the mid-1990s alone.

In interpreting the meaning of archaeology as currently depicted in newspapers, a few preliminaries are worth discussing. Most important, it is dangerous to assume that just because academics are used (and expected) to evaluate texts on the basis of their written content rather than their headlines or images, newspaper readers do the same. Concerning newspaper reporting about ongoing excavations, a Swedish archaeologist expressed to me his view that headlines only function to catch the reader's attention, and that it is the main content of the article that matters most and can be best influenced by archaeologists. More important, he went on, than getting the story right is to motivate journalists to return to the site later and report about it again, giving archaeologists the chance gradually to get across their story. Arguably, however, this view is naive considering the decisive importance of the chosen headline – and associated images – in determining the specific character, appeal and relevance of the entire story (cf. Kulik 2003a). Headlines and images reveal most clearly the meaning of archaeology in topical newspaper articles. Regarding the brand of archaeology they are far more significant than the main content of the article.

Even a cursory look at archaeological news headlines reveals directly some of the main cultural meanings of archaeology in popular culture. Excluding the very many straight news items and reports about current events or topical political decisions, many headlines of archaeological stories refer to one of four themes: an interesting discovery, a mystery solved, on-going detective work or a new scholarly insight (see also Högberg 2004). Newspaper journalists are inclined to try and catch the readers' interests by referring to tried-and-tested themes, even if they are clichés. As on TV, archaeology in newspapers is increasingly becoming "archaeotainment" (Kapff 2004).

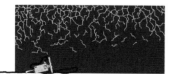

Archaeological news headlines from around the world (20 April 2004)[25]:

Ancient inscribed slab brought to light (IOL.com)
Vast and Deadly Fleets May Yield Secrets at Last (New York Times)
Technology speeds up efforts to piece together ancient marble map of Rome (Stanford Report)
What made humans modern? The urge to adorn, scholars say (Boston Globe)
Group on quest to recreate Zheng He's ship (Straits Times)
Curtain raised on mysterious ancient ethnic regime in NW China (Xinhuanet)
Golden Boadicea necklet found (BBC News)
Scientists Win New Battle Over Skeleton (Associated Press/Yahoo News)

The reason for this is simple. In a highly competitive news market, newspaper articles need not only to cover *current news* but especially *relevant* current news. The German archaeologists Marion Benz and Anna Liedmeier (forthcoming) argued that relevant to readers is what they perceive to be close to them. That proximity to readers can be spatial and thus achieved by concentrating on local and regional news or by giving stories a local or regional touch (e.g. "Munich archaeologists ... in the Euphrates valley"; see also figure on p. 48). But proximity can also be affective and lead to stories being given an emphasis either on topics people are currently interested in (e.g. since 11 September 2001, ancient terrorism or archaeology and war), or on charismatic individuals readers can identify with (e.g. by focussing on Tutankhamen rather than Egyptian archaeology). Affective proximity can also be created by using terms like "sensational", "spectacular" or superlatives like "first", "oldest", "biggest", as they will automatically create the perception that the story is relevant. Generally, archaeological news stories will be perceived as interesting and worth reading – not when they present something genuinely new and original – but when they relate to the reader's own position and their existing preferences, i.e. what they already know. These are general trends that relate to all newspaper reporting, not just to archaeological or scientific stories (Gregory and Miller 1998: 110-17). For science journalism is primarily journalism.

The Swedish archaeologist Stig Welinder (1987) conducted an analysis of all references to archaeology in four Swedish and Norwegian newspapers during the year of 1985, choosing one national and one regional paper in each country. His results demonstrated that most articles focus on only a few aspects of their work, namely fieldwork, handling of finds,

---

[25] compiled using http://www.archaeologica.org/NewsPage.htm

Archaeological stories in German newspaper. Two characteristic examples. Top: *Leipziger Volkszeitung, Delitzsch* (31 May 2002) titling "Three graves discovered within a Slavic settlement" (reproduced by kind permission of Leipziger Volkszeitung, www.lvz-online.de). Bottom: *Bildzeitung Dresden* (7 August 2002) titling "Dresden Stonehenge discovered: Stone Age observatory is 7000 years old!"

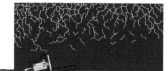

cultural heritage management and the presentation of research results. He summed up his findings like this (1987: 36, 130; my translation):

"The characteristic archaeologist is active in the cultural landscape, at heritage or excavation sites, or in museum archives and exhibitions. Archaeologists have things in their hands: a spade, a drawing-board, artefacts. At the same time, the archaeologist is a theoretician and expert, an expert for prehistoric and early historical people and societies, for the preservation and restoration of the cultural landscape, for ancient ways of life and techniques."

"Expectations for archaeological fieldwork are about an exciting hunt for sensational finds and treasures. With the help of shovels and spades and sensible technical equipment, the archaeologist penetrates into the unknown, the mystical and the mysterious."

Recently, Stig Welinder (1997) and Anders Högberg (2004) basically confirmed these results in the light of new studies of Swedish newspapers reporting about archaeology.

Newspaper images, too, tend to show archaeologists working on site as well as particular finds, thus corresponding to the association of "digging up things" which people have when they hear the word "archaeology" (as discussed in chapter 4). Indeed, more space can be given to the images than to the text. Archaeological images grab attention, they convey emotions and atmosphere, they appeal aesthetically, they have the ability to illustrate complex circumstances (Benz and Liedmeier forthcoming).

An analysis I carried out of all print media articles (including some print-outs from online sources) published about archaeology in the German state of Saxonia in 2002 yielded some interesting figures. Although one in three, often short, reports were picture-less, those with pictures showed most frequently archaeologists at work (35%) and particular finds (26%), sometimes held by the archaeologist in charge, with another 12% being photographs of the archaeological site as such. Almost one in every four articles contained more than one image, often mixing the most popular motifs.

These major trends were also born out in Bodil Petersson's (1994) study of newspaper articles about the Swedish site of Birka (see chapter 7). Many of the headlines of her sample referred to the process of digging up Viking Age treasures of one sort or another. In terms of illustrations, again, approximately one third of the associated images showed

archaeologists at work in the field and another quarter depicted individual finds. The journalist Neal Ascherson (2004: 155) suggested a possible explanation for this tendency to highlight specific discoveries. Since, by tradition, archaeology in newspapers is consigned to news pages, the reports are expected to cover events, such as new discoveries. Discussions of, for instance, carefully considered historical interpretations or their wider implications require feature articles that may appear in the culture or science sections.

Interestingly, Elisabeth Pühringer (2000: 80-1) argued that on TV, too, the most common, stereotypical images shown are those of the archaeologist squatting on the ground gradually revealing some bones or artefacts with a trowel or brush and the archaeologist on the dig site, holding or showing cleaned-up finds, talking to the camera. Newspaper stories about archaeology thus confirm the emphasis in TV programmes on the process of *doing* archaeology in the present. They all focus on archaeologists digging, finding, revealing and studying things. In particular, the image of archaeology is excavation-centred. As Welinder commented (1987: 157), what is lacking is – paradoxically – a historical time perspective.

Newspaper reports thus do not predominantly educate about the past but celebrate the work of archaeologists mainly in terms of clue-hunting, discoveries, mysteries and revelations (see also Högberg 2004; cf. chapter 5). This is what draws readers, what makes an archaeological story relevant to them. I have not been able to discern any notable differences of that trend between the U.K., Sweden and Germany. It is important to realise in this context that I do not claim that newspaper readers are not interested in anything other than stereotypical headlines and images. What I am arguing is that they appear to be *especially* interested in archaeology when it is presented in *this* way. Could that have anything to do with what people generally are thinking about archaeology?

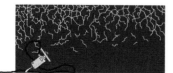

Chapter 4

What people are thinking about archaeology

When I told colleagues that I was investigating the meaning of archaeology in contemporary popular culture, many thought immediately that I was interviewing people. Popular culture is however not identical with people's perceptions or beliefs – although they can be reflected in popular culture.

Nevertheless, I would have loved to obtain some new empirical data of how people actually perceive archaeology and archaeologists. Unfortunately I did not succeed in getting the necessary funding. This chapter will therefore briefly review several surveys with results relevant to my study that were conducted by others. Unfortunately the amount of such existing research is very limited. The British archaeologist Nick Merriman (2004: 8) is right in stating that archaeologists have largely been "communicating blindly to an audience they do not understand, and [that] it is no wonder that so many attempts at communicating archaeology result in boredom or incomprehension."

A small number of polls and surveys investigating public attitudes towards archaeology and archaeological heritage have however been carried out, mostly over the past decade. In Sweden, a representative survey of the adult Swedish population was conducted in 2002, carrying the title "What does the cultural environment mean to you?" (Statistiska Centralbyrån 2002). Its aims were broadly similar to English Heritage's representative study of attitudes towards heritage among adults in England (English Heritage 2000). Both projects related to heritage in general and particularly to the situation in their respective countries. The English survey contained no questions relating specifically to archaeological issues.

Polls and surveys that were specifically geared towards archaeological issues include

- Nick Merriman's postal survey of behaviour and attitudes concerning heritage, museums and the past among a representative sample of British adults (Merriman 1991),
- Lisa Mackinney's interviews about archaeology with a relatively small number of

visitors of the California Academy of Sciences (Mackinney 1994a, 1994b),

- David Pokotylo's co-authored reports, based on questionnaires distributed by his students, about public attitudes towards archaeological resources and their management in the greater Vancouver area (Pokotylo and Mason 1991; Pokotylo and Guppy 1999),
- The Society for American Archaeology's representative survey of adult Americans about public perceptions and attitudes about archaeology (Ramos and Duganne 2000),
- a survey of attitudes concerning archaeology and the past in Germany, conducted by a group of students from the universities of Bonn and Cologne (Bohne and Heinrich 2000; see Postscriptum p.61).
- David Pokotylo's research about attitudes towards the archaeological heritage among a representative sample of the Canadian population (Pokotylo 2002),
- and a number of other, either very specific or fairly informally conducted local surveys (e.g. Paynton 2002; Högberg 2004).

Some interesting insights from these existing surveys are relevant also to the argument of this book.

The single most significant source of information about archaeology is TV.

The Swedish survey (Statistiska Centralbyrån 2002) found that 83% of all Swedes watch TV-programmes about history. The interviewees were also asked whether they had ever received information about an archaeological excavation and, if they had, where this information came from. Seventy per cent answered "Yes, from radio or TV", with an additional 60% stating "Yes, from articles in newspapers or magazines." Only 2% received information from the Internet. The survey also concluded that 22% of the 6 million adult Swedes (and 32% of those with higher education) know about archaeological excavation from guided tours at excavation sites. However, when the Swedes were asked where they would be looking for additional information about an archaeological excavation or find, 41% pointed to the Internet (58% of those with higher education), 37% to newspapers or magazines, 34% to libraries and only 16% to radio or TV. The discrepancy between the actual influence and the ascribed potential of the Internet would support the hypothesis that for the most part, the Swedes do not search for additional information about archaeological excavations and are content with the information they already receive.

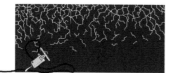

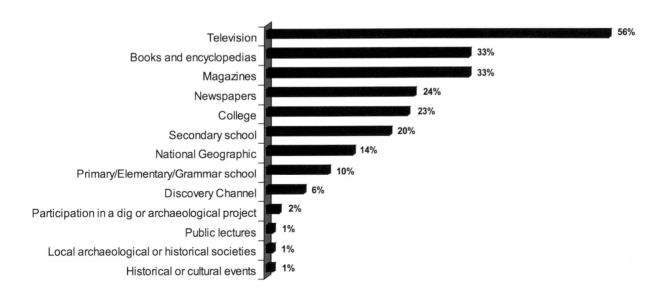

Television	56%
Books and encyclopedias	33%
Magazines	33%
Newspapers	24%
College	23%
Secondary school	20%
National Geographic	14%
Primary/Elementary/Grammar school	10%
Discovery Channel	6%
Participation in a dig or archaeological project	2%
Public lectures	1%
Local archaeological or historical societies	1%
Historical or cultural events	1%

What are the sources of information through which you have learned about archaeology?
Data from: Ramos and Duganne 2000.

The American survey (Ramos and Duganne 2002) confirmed the huge significance of TV as the main source of information about archaeology. It concluded that 56% of adult Americans learn about archaeology from TV, followed by magazines (33%) and books (33%) and newspapers (24%). When asked where they would like to learn about archaeology, the Americans confirmed the relative significance of the media as it already exists (TV 50%, magazines 22%, books 21%, newspapers 11%).

In Canada too, TV seems to be most common source of archaeological knowledge (Pokotylo and Mason 1991). Concerning the question where they had learned about prehistoric archaeology, 81% of the (not representative) sample selected *Television*, followed by *Magazines* (66%), *Books* (59%), *Newspapers* (47%), *Courses* (47%) and *Movies* (30%!) from a given list of possible answers. More than two out of three replied that they would like to see more information on prehistoric archaeology made available to the general public. This group was then asked where they would like to receive additional information. On another pre-selected list, they chose most often *Television*

OLD
POTS
£1

(77%). Interestingly though, 68% would like to receive more information on archaeology from *Museum exhibits* and 66% would like to learn more by *Visiting an archaeological dig*. Any interpretation of the unusual preference for museums must take into account that, in exchange for returning the survey forms, respondents were offered free admission to the local University Museum of Anthropology. We do not know if they were regular museum visitors anyway.

Another, later study by Pokotylo and his students (Pokotylo and Guppy 1999) enquired about sources of existing archaeological knowledge too. This was the only survey where *Television* came second (55%) after *Museums* (58%), with *Travel* ranking third (37%). When asked, how they would like to learn more about archaeology, the same sample indicated similar preferences, though with TV in front again: *Television* (68%), *Travel* (62%) and *Museums* (58%). The popularity of museums and travel is striking. The fact that respondents had immediately before been asked whether information on archaeological research was "accessible" to them (so that they were perhaps already thinking about going places) and that most of those responding were middle-aged, well educated Euro-Canadians who, once again, were promised free admission to the University Museum of Anthropology in return for submitting the questionnaire may go some way in contextualising these answers.

A large, recent Canadian survey (Pokotylo 2002) found that in terms of perceived effectiveness of learning about archaeology (on a scale from 0 to 10), *watching TV/movies* had the same level of approval as *reading books/magazines* (7.2) and came after *travelling to actual archaeological sites* (8.1) and *attending a college/university* (7.6) but before *surfing the Internet* (6.9).

A fairly small survey undertaken in the UK, confirmed the dominating significance of TV in informing people about archaeology (Paynton 2002).

The most common association people have with "archaeology" is digging up things.

The American survey (Ramos and Duganne 2002) began by asking the open question "What do you think of when you hear the word 'archaeology'?" The single most common association was with *Digging*. All associations with digging in some form or other (including

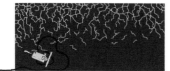

- "Archaeology? Digging? That's only the half of it ....
there's also troweling, mattocking, barrowing, backfilling,
shoring, sectioning, shovelling, draining, de-turfing...."

Digging artefacts or *bones*) amount to a full 59%. Associations with particular finds form a second group: *Dinosaurs/Dinosaur bones* (10%), *Bones* (9%), *Artefacts* (8%). The past itself was not explicitly associated all that often: *History, heritage and antiquity* (12%), *Ancient cultures and civilizations* (8%).

The most recent Canadian survey (Pokotylo 2002) began likewise with an open question about associations with the word "archaeology" and came to broadly similar results. *Excavations/Digs* were the single most popular association (39%), followed by particular kinds of finds: *Sites/ruins/artefacts* (29%), *Dinosaur bones/fossils* (21%), *Dinosaurs* (17%), *Human bones* (10%). Near the bottom of the list were associations with the past as such: *Ancient past* (14%), *Heritage/History* (13%).

An earlier Canadian study asked a very similar question but categorised the answers in a slightly different way (Pokotylo and Guppy 1999). Again, various ways of doing archaeology were most often associated with archaeology. *Study the past using archaeological record, methods* was the most popular association (21%), with *Excavations* being very common too (17%). 20% associated *Study the past, ancient society, civilizations* and

Survey	Most common	2nd most common	3rd most common
Ramos and Duganne 2002	Digging (22%)	History, heritage and antiquity (12%)	Digging artefacts/things/objects from the past (11%)
Pokotylo 2002	Excavations/Digs (39%)	Sites/ruins/artefacts (29%)	Dinosaur bones/fossils (21%)
Pokotylo and Guppy 1999	Study the past using archaeological record, methods (21%)	Study the past, ancient society, civilizations (20%)	Excavations (17%)
Mackinney 1994a	Digging (32%)	Past (28%)	Ancient civilizations/cultures (24%)
Högberg 2004	Excavating/excavation tools (26%)	Finding ancient artefacts (16%)	Investigating (9%) Ancient cultures (9%)
Merriman 1991	The Past (62%)	Ruins or Objects (53%)	Digging (45%)

The most popular associations with "archaeology"

11% *Antiquity/history/heritage,* but here only 9% of the answers were classified as associating *Artefacts/sites/ruins.*

A similar trend was shown in Lisa Mackinney's interviews (Mackinney 1994a). When her sample of visitors of the California Academy of the Sciences was asked what came to mind when they heard the word "archaeology", many, again, referred to *Digging* (32%). In this case, associations with the past came second: *Past* (28%), *Ancient civilizations/cultures* (24%). Specific kinds of finds and individual sites trailed the list: *Fossils* (20%), *Bones* (18%), *Buildings* (12%), *Artefacts* (10%), *Specific sites in Egypt* (10%).

This was broadly confirmed also by Anders Högberg's (2004) survey of 50 adults in southern Sweden. He, too, asked about associations with archaeology and received most frequently answers referring to *excavating/excavation tools* (26%), followed by *finding ancient artefacts* (16%), *investigating/researching* (9%) and references to specific *ancient cultures* (9%). References to *the past* generally were made in 7% of the supplied answers. Interestingly, Högberg was also able to confirm an earlier study (André et al 2001) which argued that the interest in archaeological fieldwork can come in two different forms that merge in the image of the digging archaeologist. On the one hand, there is

a fascination with its exotic, strange and thrilling aspects and on the other hand, there is an even more popular fascination with the down-to-earth and craft-like character of archaeology. The overall trend that archaeology is predominantly associated with a particular research process, particularly digging/excavation, is confirmed by all these studies.

The only exception from this trend I am aware of is Nick Merriman's British survey. He asked respondents on his questionnaire to "write down what the word 'Archaeology' means" to them and then categorised the wide range of answers given. Most frequently mentioned were *The Past* (62%), *Ruins* or *Objects* (53%), followed by *Digging* (45%) and *Study* or *Research* (43%). *Discovery* received mentionings by as few as 10% of the sample (Merriman 1991: 98). I cannot possibly guess why these answers show such a different pattern, although it has to be said that in absolute terms the proportion of respondents associating archaeology with digging is not lower but actually higher than in the other surveys.

Being asked specifically, in an open question, what archaeologists "do" in their work, more than a third of the Californian visitors (38%) stated again that they *Dig* (Mackinney 1994a). The next popular responses were *Use artefacts to piece together how ancient cultures or civilizations lived* (26%), *Find artefacts* (24%) and *Work hard* (18%!). When asked a similar open question, the American adults, too, emphasised, through a wide variety of answers given, that archaeologists are digging and discovering archaeological sites, artefacts or bones, or uncovering ancient civilizations (Ramos and Duganne 2002). However, the single most common answer was *Analyzing and researching the past to discover and learn what life/past civilizations were like* (25%). It is impossible to tell though whether the answers subsumed under this category actually meant "learning about the human past" or rather "discovering secrets of ancient civilizations", or whether they may have been deliberately ambiguous in that respect. Whereas the former alternative could be taken to refer to a genuine interest in knowledge derived from academic scholarship, the second might suggest instead a fascination with revealing lost treasures and ancient mysteries. Although this distinction may not be one people make themselves, the two interests are not identical (see chapter 5).

In a subsequent question, all those American adults who had earlier acknowledged an interest in the past (76%), were then asked the open question what it was that interested them personally about archaeology. Forty five per cent stated that they were

interested in learning about the human past and how people lived, 18% mentioned history and only 14% referred to the thrill and sense of discovery, 12% to finding old things and another 12% to ancient civilizations.

This result should not though be taken uncritically as indication for a strong interest in academic modes of knowledge about the past. In questions that impinge on educational norms and social status, there is always a problem with people's self-assessments due to a tendency to try and meet expectations of the interviewer. (When first asked how interested you are in archaeology and you were happy to signal some or even considerable interest, you may immediately afterwards feel compelled to qualify this interest by saying that you are interested in learning about the past. Referring to discovering treasures and solving mysteries could be perceived as disqualifying what you had said first.)

When a Canadian sample of households was asked to specify what archaeologists do (Pokotylo and Mason 1991), the two answers most commonly selected were *Study lifeways of past cultures* (64%) and *Excavation of valuable art objects* (43%). Here again, I am unsure as to what this tells us in relation to the perception of archaeology and archaeologists. The pre-formulated answers do not allow to distinguish clearly between "learning about the human past" (the archaeologist as scholar), "excavating artefacts of past cultures" (the archaeologist as detective or collector) and "discovering treasures" (the archaeologist as adventurer and treasure hunter).

People enjoy "doing" archaeology themselves.

I mentioned earlier a very high figure of adult Swedes (22%) who say they have taken part in guided tours on excavation. I also reported that about half of a total (not representative) sample of Canadian households and more than two thirds of those who would like more information about prehistoric archaeology be made widely available, would prefer this additional information to be conveyed by *Visiting an archaeological dig* (Pokotylo and Mason 1991). Both results may be related to the widespread desire of observing archaeologists in action. By the same token, Lisa Mackinney's interviews suggested that her Californian sample of visitors was very keen to learn more about archaeological techniques. When asked what they would expect to do, see, feel and find out about in an exhibit about archaeology, they had the following main expectations,

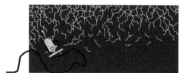

which may partly overlap with their own interests (as indicated by Mackinney 1994b): *Archaeological techniques and tools* (34%), *Artefacts* (28%), *Digging* (18%), *Hands-on* (18%).

On the question whether they themselves had ever done what archaeologists do, 6% of the same visitors said they had been involved in *Digging*. According to the American survey (Ramos and Duganne 2002), 4.5% of all adult Americans claim to have already participated in an archaeological dig – a figure that strikes me as very high since it amounts to almost 10 million people! Interestingly, in one of the Canadian studies (Pokotylo and Guppy 1999), nearly exactly the same proportion of people stated that they had participated in an archaeological excavation. Maybe both figures simply reflect a very wide definition of "participation".

- "That's the last time 'C' Wing are going to be given archaeology club privileges!"

At any rate, more realistic seems to be that 10% of the adult Americans would like to participate in an archaeological dig or other kind of archaeological project in the future. This is the equivalent of more than 20 million people. If the interest was the same in Europe – and there is no reason to expect a smaller figure – we are talking about 45 million people inside the European Union and more than 65 million people across the entire continent who would like to participate in an archaeological project.

These figures may not be unbelievably high. Several surveys Channel 4 conducted among viewers of the incredibly successful British TV series *Time Team*, established that over 80% of its

OLD POTS £1

"Ordinarily, Gregory hated digging. Mud and rain; lunch in cold, draughty huts; hands and knees work; muddy boots and treacherous duck-boards. [...] Still, there was always the fascination of the finds. At least there had always been that. To hold something in your hand immediately after its retrieval from a subterranean limbo, to establish some kind of direct bridge with the person who had lost it or thrown it away or made it, however many years before, that was quite something. Even Gregory had to admit that. He didn't even really have to admit it, it was what had brought him to archaeology in the first place. Fitting the pieces together, like a jigsaw. Sometimes quite literally like a jigsaw."

Richard Jenkins, *The Archaeologist* (1998: 94)

audience (more than 3 million people in the UK) would like to "learn all about the processes involved in archaeology and do some practical excavation".[26]

Discussion

Most of the existing surveys did not look specifically at how archaeology and archaeologists are depicted in people's minds but had other aims. Some of the cited results were therefore of a fairly general nature. Others were inconclusive as to their precise implications for the interest of this study. In practice, the existing studies investigated mostly one (or more) of three issues:

(1) public awareness and support for site preservation, for aboriginal claims to archaeological sites or finds, or for archaeology generally (incl. teaching and funding);

(2) the extent to which popular knowledge about the past, heritage management (incl. legislation) and archaeology generally are accurate and realistic;

(3) basic social parameters about visitors, sources of information about archaeological knowledge etc.

These issues are doubtlessly significant in their own right. The results of the surveys cited can serve to develop more effective means of communicating to the public about archaeology, improving education about both the past, the ownership or the best management of archaeological heritage and increasing the support base for archaeological research and site preservation.

My own interest and the perspective taken in this book are different though and I am not concerned with gauging public support for archaeology or preservation, evaluating

---

[26] http://www.channel4.com/history/microsites/B/bigdig/archaeologist/faqs.html#doit

the accuracy of popular beliefs about archaeology or heritage, or establishing basic demographic and sociological facts about visitors and their knowledge. Instead, this work's focus is on attitudes about archaeology as reflected in popular culture. Surprisingly, this field has not yet attracted a great amount of empirical attention. Ironically, although archaeologists are usually obsessed with context in the past, the cultural and social context of archaeology itself is still little known. As Nick Merriman (2004: 15) recently argued, "archaeologists have until recently not treated their relationship with the public as something which merited their academic attention." He went on to state that it is time now to study that relationship with the same degree of rigour as archaeologists study societies of the past.

In chapter 7, I will be discussing some of the wider implications of the issues discussed in this chapter. Before that, I need to delve deeper into the main themes characterising the meaning of archaeology in popular culture and the main strategies available to professional archaeologists of engaging with these themes.

Postscriptum: Another survey became available to me only after the present manuscript was already completed (Bohne and Heinrich 2000). Although this German study acknowledges its methodological limitations, it provides at the same time interesting additional data concerning the perceptions among the German public of archaeology and archaeologists.

Chapter 5

The archaeologist in popular culture: key themes

This chapter reviews the most important perceptions of archaeology and archaeologists in contemporary popular culture. One of the most important insights that will emerge is that the archaeology is largely perceived in positive terms. The archaeologist is seen as a hero and role model, competent and resourceful, through new discoveries and important revelations serving the interests of society and occasionally of humanity. This is an important, though often underappreciated asset for professional archaeologists and their discipline.

Other academic fields start out from very different positions. Almost two decades ago, George Gerbner (1987), an American Professor of Communications, concluded in his research about science on television that science and scientists were generally less positively portrayed in prime-time television drama than other professions. Indeed, scientists often fail: "about 5 percent of the scientists portrayed on television kill someone and 10 percent get killed" (Gerbner 1987: 111). That, Gerbner went on, is the highest victimization rate of any occupational group on TV, including private investigators, police and the army! Likewise, in her comprehensive research about representations of scientists in Western Literature, the Australian Professor of English, Roslynn Haynes (1994) found that literary representations, like many surveys among people, tend to portray scientists in broadly negative terms and sometimes they are even seen as evil and dangerous. Similarly, Diane Bjorklund (2001), an American sociologist, found that the vast majority of eighty twentieth century novels containing portrayals of sociologists presented unfavourable images. In almost none of them is the sociologist a particularly likeable character. Archaeology, on the other hand, is one of the few disciplines with a largely positive image.

As far as movies are concerned, a recent study of 222 films concluded that the "strongest genre among films about science is the horror movie", whereas "there are hardly any comedies about science" (Weingart et al 2003: 286). Archaeology has not inspired many comedies either (although there are some notable exceptions such as the Swedish *Den ofrivilliga golfaren* [1991] and the British *Carry On Behind* [1975]). But archaeology's image has certainly benefited a lot from archaeologists as heroes in popular movies such as *Pimpernel*

Smith (1941), *The Purple Rose of Cairo* (1985) and the recent *Indiana Jones* (1981, 1984, 1989), *Stargate* (1994) and *Lara Croft* (2001, 2003) films – although the field has also its share of horror movies, especially such concerning nasty mummies.

The themes archaeologists are associated with in popular culture can be divided into four main categories: the archaeologist as adventurer; the archaeologist as detective; the archaeologist making profound revelations; and the archaeologist taking care of ancient sites and finds. These themes are characteristic

for the contemporary Western world, although it is clear that they have roots that go back at least as far as the 19th century (Bray 1981; Zintzen 1998; Russell 2002b). In the remainder of this chapter I will discuss each of these themes in turn. I hasten to add that I am of course aware that others have proposed alternative categorisations (see e.g. Ascher 1960; Bray 1981; Stern and Tode 2002; Russell 2002b; Hendriks 2005; Sandberg 2006; see also Holtorf 2004). These alternatives are not necessarily incompatible with my own attempt but I found nevertheless that the present study required some modifications that finally led to a new scheme.

The A theme: the archaeologist as Adventurer

There can be no doubt that throughout popular culture the theme of adventure is the single most important association with archaeology. It is hardly surprising that a new popular archaeology magazine in Germany has been called *Abenteuer Archäologie*. *The History Channel* promises accordingly about its new archaeological TV series *Digging for the Truth*: "it's not just archaeology, it's an adventure!"[27] Archaeology has come to stand

---

[27] http://www.historychannel.com/diggingforthetruth

for a quest involving travel to exotic locations, simple living and working conditions in the field, unexpected tests and dangers, followed by spectacular discoveries, recovery of treasures and the successful return home of the virtuous hero – all forming parts of essential adventure stories (Zarmati 1995; Holtorf 2005: chapters 2+3).

The essential adventure story

The heroic adventure story is an archetypical narrative structure that can be found in many rituals and a wide variety of world literature, including epics, fairy tales, myths, religious tales and film scripts. Joseph Campbell's classic account significantly bears the title *The Hero With a Thousand Faces* (1988 [1949]). These faces include those of Odysseus, Jesus, Buddha, Heinrich Schliemann, Rocky, Thor Heyerdahl, Indiana Jones, *Stargate*'s Daniel Jackson and Lara Croft, among many others.

The adventurous journey of the hero always features the same stages of separation, initiation and return: (1) The hero leaves home in order to embark on a quest into the unknown; (2) the hero is tested and subjected to all sorts of (possibly supernatural) ordeals but also encounters helpers and eventually triumphs in a spectacular way; and (3) the hero returns as a transformed person after the quest has been fulfilled and something significant has been revealed. The transitions between each stage are marked by prominent threshold crossings, but throughout the entire journey the hero has moral superiority on his (or nowadays increasingly: her) side and never needs to question the mission as such.

A look at the listings on the satellite TV channel *Adventure 1* shows the variety of hero journeys that are popular today, reflecting a desire for out-of-the-ordinary experiences.[28] Beyond the screen, people enjoy reading adventure magazines (like the German P.M. magazines), visiting adventure parks (like those managed by the American corporation Anheuser-Busch), taking their kids to adventure playgrounds and adventure pools, practicing adventure sports (like climbing or mountain-biking) and going on adventure holidays to Lapland or on safari in Africa (Köck 1990). But scientific discovery is arguably the greatest of all adventures (Haynes 1994: 130). Even academic literature can resemble classic tales about hero adventures (Atkinson 1996: chapter 5). Indeed, the scientist as heroic adventurer is one of six recurring archetypes of scientists in Western literature:

"Towering like a superman over his contemporaries, exploring new territories, or engaging with new concepts, this character emerges at periods of scientific optimism. His particular appeal to adolescent audiences, deriving from the implicit promise of transcending boundaries, whether material, social, or intellectual, has ensured the popularity of this stereotype in comics and space opera. More subtle analyses of such heroes, however, suggest the danger of their charismatic power as, in the guise of neo-imperialist space travellers, they impose their particular brand of colonization on the universe." (Haynes 1994: 3)

---

[28] http://www.sky.com/skycom/tvguide/0,,544-0,00.html

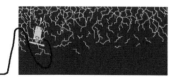

The associations of archaeology with adventure are as old as archaeology itself. In a famous passage written more than three decades before Indiana Jones, the American archaeologist Alfred Kidder (1949: XI) argued that

"In popular belief, and unfortunately to some extent in fact, there are two sorts of archaeologists, the hairy-chested and the hairy-chinned. [The hairy-chested variety appears] as a strong-jawed young man in a tropical helmet, pistol on hip, hacking his way through the jungle in search of lost cities and buried treasure. His boots, always highly polished, reach to his knees, presumably for protection against black mambas and other sorts of deadly serpents. The only concession he makes to the difficulties and dangers of his calling is to have his shirt enough unbuttoned to reveal the manliness of his bosom."

The A-theme has often been employed to tell the stories both of archaeologists' research in the present and of the history of archaeology (see also chapters 2 and 3). In this view, the archaeologist is an uncompromising adventurer and explorer who conquers ancient sites and artefacts and earns just rewards for pushing forward the frontiers of our knowledge about the past. Some scenes of TV documentaries have reminded critics even of takes usually associated with war movies (Stern and Tode 2002: 80).

Stereotypes associated with adventure very much inform the image of archaeologists in children's toys (e.g. Playmobil, cf. Holtorf 2005: fig 3.3), comic series (e.g. Indiana Jöns in Donald Duck comics), contemporary advertising (Talalay 2004: 211), literary fiction (e.g. Preston and Child 1999), private museums (e.g. Thor Heyerdahl's Kon-Tiki Museum in Oslo[29]), computer games[30], films (Stern 2002; Day 1997: 18; Membury 2002; Russell 2002b) as well as in widely read magazines like *National Geographic Magazine* (with national sub-editions in Germany and Sweden), among other areas of popular culture. In particular, the clothes in which archaeologists appear often reveal intended associations with heroic adventures (see below).

Unfortunately these kinds of clichés and narratives are not always harmless entertainment but can have highly problematic colonial and imperial undertones, as most of the entries in my catalogue exemplify (see also Cohodas 2003; Hall 2004). With particular regard to *National Geographic*, it has been argued (Gero and Root 1990: 34) that the magazine:

---

[29] http://www.kon-tiki.no
[30] http://www.4players.de/rendersite.php?LAYOUT=showthema&THEMAID=8&SYSTEM=Spielkultur

"has played an active role in promulgating a nationalist ideology, presenting a view of the past that promotes technological progress as cultural superiority, [American] expansionism as scientific inquiry for the benefit of humankind, and democratic state systems as inevitable and normative outgrowths of the great civilizations of the ancient Western world."

This criticism can be generalised and applied to very many archaeologists portrayed according to the conventions of the A theme, including Indiana Jones himself. Recalling "imperial adventure tales for boys", the famous film trilogy with Harrison Ford in the lead role is premised on "an imperialized globe, in which archeology professors can 'rescue' artefacts from the colonized world for the greater benefit of science and civilization" (Shohat and Stam 1994: 124). Still worse, in the movie *March or Die* (1977) Max von Sydow plays the scrupulous archaeologist François Marneau who is trying to secure an ancient Moroccan treasure at all cost. He is quite ready to sacrifice human lives and peace with the Arab tribes for what he – misguidedly – considers the greater good of archaeology. Underlying the German board game *Lost Cities* (1999) appears to be a similar narrative. The game involves "gripping expeditions" into "remote and mysterious corners of the earth", with images showing white men betting about the "success" of their expeditions to snowed-under ruins in the Himalaya, Mesoamerican sculptures in the jungle and Egyptian ruins in the desert, among other places. The aim of the game is to maximise the "glory" of each expedition (all my translations). Only rarely – as in the *Mummy* films – does the archaeologist have to face the consequences of his doings...

Adventurer-archaeologists of popular culture:		
Lara Croft	The heroine of the computer game and *Tomb Raider* films	www.tombraider.com; www.cubeit.com/ctimes
Rick Dangerous	The hero of a classic computer game	www.rickdangerous.co.uk
Professor Sydney Fox, historian in the Department of Ancient Studies	The heroine of the TV-series *Relic Hunter*	www.relichunter.tk

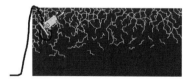

Professor Indiana Jones	The hero in novels by various authors and three films by George Lucas and Steven Spielberg	www.theindyexperience.com; www.indianajones.com
Indiana Pipps, Indiana Ding, Indiana Goof, Indiana Jöns, Arizona Goof, etc.	Goofy's cousin who appears in Disney's *Donald Duck* stories under various names in different countries	stp.ling.uu.se/~starback/dcml/chars/arizona.html
Will Rock	The hero of a computer game	en.wikipedia.org/wiki/Will_Rock
Professor Robson	The hunky professor in the soft-porn film series *The Adventures of Justine* (1995-6)	rarevideos.bravepages.com/justine.htm
Professor Bernice Summerfield	The heroine of several novels by various authors, originally part of *Doctor Who*	www.bernicesummerfield.co.uk; www.bigfinish.com/benny
Vash	character in the TV series Star Trek	www.startrek.com/startrek/view/library/character/bio/1112729.html

Occasionally archaeologists in popular culture are simply greedy themselves or tempted by the market value of their finds, so that they decide to seek personal fortune from their work, although they do not all conform with the A theme entirely (see Maier-Maidl and Stipper-Lackner 1997; Russell 2002b: 39). The American TV game-show *Legends of the Hidden Temple* (Nickelodeon, 1993-6), for example, involved a race of the participating childrens teams through an elaborate obstacle course evoking ruins in the jungle, in order to retrieve an artefact from "Olmec's Temple". In order to succeed they needed to bribe several "native" Temple Guards along the way. In the film *Deceived* (1991) museum curator Jack Saunders sells precious ancient artefacts from his own collection. These are examples for what the American archaeologist Barbara Little has called "Artifact Lust" (1991: 25).

As shown in a brilliant analysis by the Austrian writer and German literature specialist Christiane Zintzen (1998: chapter 7), a particularly well-suited template for such archaeological narratives has been the life and career of Heinrich Schliemann (1822-1890). Like few others, he personified both to himself and to others the lonely hero on a long journey. Despite being an outsider, he knew 'the truth' – in this case about the historical reality of Homer's Troy – early on but was ridiculed until he finally embarked on his quest alone and under great difficulties. In the end, however, Schliemann, like the archetypal hero, proved himself right by making great discoveries, becoming accepted as scholars and celebrated as a national hero. Many have since then drawn inspiration and motivation from this truly mythical story, so that one may even speak of a "Schliemann Effect" (Membury 2002: 18).

Best-selling accounts of archaeological romances involving mystery, adventure and hardship but concluding with the reward of treasure were pioneered by the author Kurt W. Marek (1915-1972) alias C. W. Ceram who published in 1949 his instant classic *Götter, Gräber und Gelehrte* (Gods, Graves and Scholars). This book tells the story of the 'great' archaeological adventures and discovery processes in the eastern Mediterranean, Egypt, the Middle East and Central America by focussing on the archaeologist heroes themselves. Among them are the celebrities Heinrich Schliemann, Arthur Evans, Howard Carter and Leonard Woolley. The appeal of this subject was such that *Götter, Gräber und Gelehrte* has been translated into 30 languages and sold approximately 5 million copies worldwide (Oels 2005: 345). The success of Ceram's writing lies in a mixture of facts and exciting storytelling where the readers suffer with their heroes until their eventual successes. It may have been that genre that led the Italian archaeologist Massimo Pallottino (1968: 231) to make the generalised statement that in the biographies of archaeologists, "the story of their adventures sometimes reads like a novel and in any case is full of moving and exciting episodes."

The use of numerous historical details and the frequent allusions to archaeology continuously advancing our knowledge by deciphering more and more of the past, became key elements of a new literary genre. So we have the *archäologischer Tatsachenroman*, or fact-based archaeological novel (Schörken 1995: 71-81; Oels 2005). This genre was very successfully continued by Geoffrey Bibby, Rudolf Pörtner, Philipp Vandenberg and Rudolf Drößler among others. Maybe unsurprisingly, when the new German magazine *Abenteuer Archäologie* was launched in 2004, its editor, Reinhard Breuer, stated in the editorial that his own interest in archaeology was woken too by Ceram's writing.

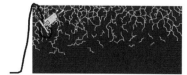

"If adventure has a name, it must be Indiana Jones"

The three existing Indiana Jones movies (*Raiders of the Lost Ark*, 1981; *Indiana Jones and the Temple of Doom*, 1984; *Indiana Jones and the Last Crusade*, 1989) created by George Lucas and Steven Spielberg are quintessential action/adventure films. The archaeologist hero, a young university professor, was played each time by Harrison Ford.

"Despite his professional attire, there was an underlying ruggedness about him, a sense that when he took off his coat and tie and ventured out into the 'field' in search of ancient artefacts, anything could happen and probably did. It was this mysterious air about him – as well as a certain shyness – that appealed to the co-eds who seemed to dominate his classes." (MacGregor 1989: 45)

Indiana's clothes and fearless character, the exciting storylines with many action scenes and the exotic sets – all were carefully developed to suggest classic adventure in the tradition of *King Solomon's Mines* (1950) and *Secret of the Incas* (1954). So much so that the poster to the second film proclaimed that "If adventure has a name, it must be Indiana Jones".

"Indiana Jones is the quintessential adventurer, with his leather jacket, felt hat, army satchel, three-day beard, and bullwhip, he is the ever-ready adventurer. A professor of archaeology by day, and a global grave-robber in his off-time, Indy scours the third world for the lost treasures of legend while being pursued by all types of unsavory people who would benefit from stealing the fruits of his labor. Indy's exploits skirt the borders of political conflict, with the Nazis and the Communists alike sometimes in pursuit of him." (French n.d.)

All films were international successes and led to the creation of a lot of merchandise as well as computer games, comic books, role-playing sourcebooks, a TV series and various kinds of novels for all age groups. The three films together grossed more than $1 billion at the box office alone. When Indiana Jones appeared in late December on the German TV channel ARD, they advertised that: "Christmas has been saved". In an American survey from 1994 only 10% of the respondents stated that they had not seen any of the *Indiana Jones* movies whereas 60% had seen all three (Mackinney 1994b). Indiana Jones is thus the most widely recognised and most enduring image of an archaeologist.

This incredible popularity may partly rely on the fact that "No one's got balls like Indiana Jones" as an ad in *Playboy* claimed. In a recent ranking by *Premiere Magazine* (April 2004) – two decades after the height of the cinematic Indiana Jones fever – the character still made no. 7 among "The 100 Greatest Movie Characters of All Time".

Even Disney has embraced Indiana Jones. Since 1995 Disneyland's "Adventure Land" features a ride called *Indiana Jones Adventure – Temple of the Forbidden Eye* which has proved to be extremely popular. Another ride with reference to the no.1 movie archaeologist was created in Disneyland Paris as *Indiana Jones et le temple du peril*. The British holiday park *Chessington World of Adventures* features a broadly similar though less advanced ride in its *Forbidden Kingdom* area. It carries the promising title *Tomb Blaster*.

As the German classical archaeologist Hans von Steuben (1977: 15) once observed, what Ceram did not accomplish was accomplished by the continuous boom of charter holidays. When you find an ancient sherd during your Mediterranean holidays, you sense, for one precious moment, what you think it's like to be an archaeologist on a foreign adventure. After all, as you recall from your Ceram and other popular histories of archaeology, significant discoveries are often made by chance and by amateurs... (Daniel 1964: 163; cf. Ascher 1960). If to you "the idea of exploring the ancient tombs of pharaohs sends shivers down your spine and swells a yearning in your heart", travel companies like Fodors advise you to "just go". They offer special archaeological "explorations" to far-away places where "plenty of secrets still remain hidden for modern-day explorers to unearth".[31] And for those who do not travel, there is still TV with its many archaeological documentaries (see chapter 3). On the website of the TV series *Ape to Man* broadcast by *The History Channel*, children are invited to play *The Missing Link Challenge*: "Get ready to embark on a quest that will take you across continents in search of 'The Missing Link' in human evolution. You will be tested on your endurance, skill and logic in a series of field trials and lab tests."[32] The same theme was taken even further in the channel's new series called *Digging for the Truth* featuring "explorer and survival expert" Josh Bernstein: "Whether he's rappelling into volcanoes, hiking across glaciers, or hacking through jungles, Josh is determined to unravel the world's greatest archaeological mysteries".[33] Similarly, a summary of the recent British series *Great Excavations* (Channel 4, 2000) could not have been written better by Ceram himself:

> "[The series tells] the story of the fascinating and often eccentric science of archaeology, from its beginnings in the 18th century to the present. It is a tale of chance finds and clever deduction, of private enterprise and national plunder, of romantic adventures and sheer cunning, of the hunt for mysterious ancient civilisations and the desire for invaluable objects."[34]

These story elements are also reminiscent of the adventures of Lara Croft, archaeological action heroine, that over the past decade acquired first computer game acclaim and then movie fame. To date she is the only video game character who made it onto the cover of fashion magazines and to have appeared in car commercials (French n.d.).

---

[31] http://fodors.iexplore.com (citation current on 12 August 2004)
[32] http://www.historychannel.com/apetoman/
[33] http://www.historychannel.com/diggingforthetruth/?page=host
[34] http://www.channel4.com/history/microsites/G/great_excavations

She is also the only archaeologist featuring in milk ads. Born in 1968, the character of Lara Croft is exactly three weeks younger than I am. But that is where the similarities end, since Lara's way of life consists of a lot of tomb raiding whereas mine does not. Lara can be described as a blend of Indiana Jones, James Bond and Pamela Anderson. She is portrayed as (the stereotype of) the perfect woman, combining girl power with male fantasies. Yet contrary to the way it

trowels are OK, but you can't beat a 9mm semi-automatic for day to day on-site work!

- Scenes you never see at the movies: Number 7
Lara Croft doing archaeology

might seem at first, Lara Croft arguably does not break the rule that heroic adventurers are male. Instead, she can be seen as a male protagonist in female masquerade, for her body is the only thing female about her (Zorpidu 2004). This is hardly surprising though, given that the genre of the adventure story demands stereotypically male characteristics for its heroes (Köck 1990: 39-43). On the other hand, it may be precisely these characteristics that make Lara the epitome of the empowered woman.

When they meet archaeologists, journalists are impressed by any reference to themes such as solved mysteries, sensational discoveries or urgent rescue attempts. That is what they need to hear in order to be interested and report for their audiences (Kapff 2004). The A theme creates public interest in matters that would otherwise be little else than footnotes in a day's news. For example, the German news magazine *Focus* titled its report about the discovery of a prehistoric grave by an amateur archaeologist with a quote from his son: "A dad like Indiana Jones." More recently, a newspaper introduced

71

OLD POTS £1

Hermann Parzinger, the new President of the German Archaeological Institute, in a fairly extensive article as "the German answer to Indiana Jones" who previously, in helicopters and jeeps, sought to recover lost peoples and their treasurers in remote areas of Siberia and Afghanistan (*Tagesspiegel*, 21 January 2003). Even local history is now affected by the A theme. A recent guide to the history of a South German region is billed on the back cover as presenting "fascinating discoveries" about "previously unresolved ... archaeological mysteries" which lie "immediately in front of our doorsteps" (my translation from Meyer 2002).

One aspect that is sometimes forgotten in archaeological hero-stories is their final element: the eventual downfall of the hero and his being cut down to size. Even the glory of Schliemann began to fade after his death, when questions were raised about the ownership of the artefacts he shipped out of their countries of origin. By the same token, Indiana Jones, in *Indiana Jones and the Last Crusade*, manages to get hold of the Holy Grail and save his father but in the end he cannot hold on to it and remains an ordinary mortal.

However far the A theme may stray (as my colleagues often point out) from the realities of professional archaeology, it has at least in parts been created and promoted by archaeologists themselves. It is beyond question that Heinrich Schliemann fabricated his autobiography so that his own heroic role would stand out more clearly (Zintzen 1998: 271-2). Even nowadays, archaeologists often do not hesitate to use phrases and generally represent themselves in ways that immediately evoke the A theme. The magazine of the University of Pennsylvania Museum of Archaeology and Anthropology carries the title *Expedition*. Numerous exhibitions and their catalogues appeal to visitors through the term "treasures" in their titles. A popularizing book series about the excavations at Birka in Sweden, co-authored by the main archaeologist in charge, featured titles for each volume with very high "Indiana Jones indices" emphasizing the quest for solving secrets, sensational finds and great revelations respectively (Petersson 1994: 25, 33). Similarly high indices can be found in a range of TV documentaries, as discussed in a recent Masters thesis from the University of Amsterdam entitled "The Indiana Jones Factor. The inevitability of the romantic hero in popular archaeological documentaries" (my translation; Hendriks 2005). Suzanne Hendriks shows how even academic archaeologists are widely portrayed in the manner of a visual cliché associated with Indiana Jones. By the same token, the Swedish archaeologist Göran Burenhult, who wrote a series of TV programmes and books about his archaeological

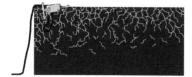

72

adventures (as discussed in chapter 3), is introduced on the dust jacket of one of the volumes (Burenhult 1986) with the words (my translation of a description he was obviously happy with):

> "To be an archaeologist is precisely as exciting as it sounds – at least if one works like Göran Burenhult. If one is an explorer of foreign cultures, then and now, whether here or on the other side of the globe."

As already mentioned (in chapter 3), the Association of German State Archaeologists greatly assisted Gisela Graichen with her TV projects (and associated books) entitled *C 14 – Advances into the Past* and *Schliemann's Heirs* – as if these titles were the most natural ones to describe their work.

Archaeologists have for a long time, even amongst themselves, considered the pleasures of fieldwork and the discovery of spectacular finds as the core of their discipline. A male archaeologist asked on an electronic discussion forum in 2004: "aren't we all (deep down) hoping to find a lost civilization, treasure hoard, gold filled tomb, find of the century? I think there is a little 'Carter' or 'Indy' in us all." [35] Paul Bahn (1989: 59) reported accordingly that it is not unusual among American archaeologists to find a bullwhip and a battered hat on the back of office-doors! Moreover, archaeological fieldwork, just like ethnographic fieldwork, certainly can be an adventurous experience (Atkinson 1996: chapter 5; Pachinko 1997; Holtorf 2005: chapter 3). A colleague of mine suspected that "the real turn-on" for archaeologists to do what they do is precisely that experience: "the finding of things, the smell of the site, the bossily-arranged lines of pegs, the sexual excitement of new people in the trench, the 'abroadness' of the places..." In this sense, it can be suggested that there is a bit of an adventurer – and a bit of an Indiana Jones – in every archaeologist.

Why Archaeology?

Because I never liked math
Because I like to feel the dirt between my hands
Because I won't be happy in an office job
Because I can drink as part of my work
Because I can feel the excitement of discovering

Archaeology is fun and interesting, one of the few disciplines that allows us to be in high ivory towers or low among the dirt. Digging kings and elites as well as digging commoners and slaves. Talking about DNA analysis or computer science as we discuss old trash and broken pots. What other discipline can offer something like this?

Alejandro Chu, abbreviated from a message sent to wac-list on 8 April 2005.

---

[35] http://www.archaeologyfieldwork.com/cgi-bin/yabb/YaBB.cgi?board=survey;action=display;num=1083202907

- "Carruthers! Good Lord! There is a time and place for your archaeology, don't you know?"

When the Swedish archaeologists Richard Holmgren and Anders Kaliff started in their own initiative (and partly with their own money) a project in Jordan, they were most deliberately in for a very special adventure. The popular account of the research conducted refers to their own "childlike enthusiasm" and "thirst for adventure" in "exotic surroundings" as "necessary ingredients" and "important motivation" of their work (Holmgren and Kaliff 2003: 151, 205, my translations). Both text and images bear witness to that thirst and enthusiasm of those two. Unfortunately all this emphasis on adventure has also resulted in gender issues being far from unimportant in the discipline (see e.g. Zarmati 1995; Moser forthcoming; Felder et al 2003: 174-177; Ransley 2005).

The A theme of popular culture has long been directly feeding back into archaeology as well. The University of Rostock, for example, incorporates the Heinrich Schliemann-Institute for Studies of the Ancient World (Heinrich Schliemann-Institut für Altertumswissenschaften). Although the name was hardly chosen to honour the adventurer Schliemann – the name Schliemann nevertheless evokes that aspect of his life too. By the same token, archaeology students I know are perfectly happy too to make reference to colourful archaeologists in popular culture. I came across email addresses such as heinrich_schliemann@web.de and lara_x_croft@hotmail.com or usernames like "relic hunter" on internet discussion forums. At least two archaeologists I have met do not object to being called "Lara Croft" by their friends.

Nowadays, many archaeology students even choose their subject out of fascination for figures like Indiana Jones. For example, Jay Fancher, a student at Washington State University, wrote to me (e-mail comm. 2003) that Indy's combination of intelligence and bravery were very appealing to him and that the seeds of his career path were planted through the association of the word 'archaeology' with adventure. The association of Indiana Jones with the academic world was explicitly fostered in 1990 by the Institute of Archaeology at University College London (David Harris, e-mail corresponence 2005). As part of a fundraising initiative to build new archaeological science laboratories at the Institute, Harrison Ford was approached and offered to donate one of Indiana Jones' bullwhips. It was subsequently auctioned for a substantial sum and the famous actor's name was recorded on a brass donors' plaque at an entrance to the labs where it recalls his generosity and is seen by passing generations of students.

The relations between the A theme and professional archaeology, then, are multi-faceted but not unproblematic. The second theme to be discussed is one that archaeology has always whole-heartedly embraced.

The D theme: the archaeologist as Detective

As contemporary Western societies are characterised by increasing specialisation, professionalisation and scientification, it is not surprising that the past too is expected to be dealt with by experts, in this case historical and archaeological scholars who have the skills to investigate the past. Archaeologists have long been considered – and considered themselves – as professional detectives of the past. They solve profound mysteries and reveal the secrets of the past for us all (Holtorf 2005: chapter 4). Alluding to this role, Alfred Kidder (1949: XI) described the opposite to the "hairy-chested" archaeologist in the following terms:

> "The hairy-chinned archaeologist [...] is old. He is benevolently absent-minded. His only weapon is a magnifying glass, with which he scrutinizes inscriptions in forgotten languages. Usually his triumphant decipherment coincides, in the last chapter, with the daughter's rescue from savages by the handsome young assistant."

The Sherlock Holmes type detective has become a common association with archae-ology. Although the detective has been associated with other disciplines too (Haynes

OLD POTS £1

The detective about the archaeologist: "Professor, you would have been a good detective."

Leslie Howard, *Pimpernel Smith* (1941)

The archaeologist about the detective: "You would have made a good archaeologist, M. Poirot. You have the gift of re-creating the past"

Agatha Christie, *Murder in Mesopotamia* (1936)

1994: 178-9), the link with archaeology is nevertheless extremely close. As has often been pointed out (e.g. Pallottino 1968: 12; Adams 1973; Gründel and Ziegert 1983; Hunter 1996), both archaeology and (forensic) criminology draw, in parts, on seemingly incontrovertible material evidence, which is carefully documented and taken to provide significant clues as to what really had happened at the site under investigation. Both use advanced technology helping them to come up with reconstructions of the past based on circumstantial evidence. An often repeated cliché is the archaeologist very patiently digging entire sites with no more than a toothbrush, for anything may be significant, how ever small.

It is not surprising that these convergences have in some cases led to close co-operation between the detectives of the past and the archaeologists of crime, for example when archaeologists have been able to assist the police in their work, producing incontrovertible evidence that would stand up in court (Hunter 1996). Vice versa, in at least one case, an archaeological mystery was attempted to be solved through a public inquiry that resembled a court trial (Darvill et al 1999). The case was the meaning of the Cerne Giant, the huge figure of a naked man cut into the chalk of a hill in Dorset, U.K. In front of a packed audience the inquiry took place on 23 March 1996 in the local Village Hall at Cerne Abbas. All was filmed by the BBC who were keen to present the debate as a courtroom drama. Three cases were presented: that the Giant is prehistoric/Romano-British in origin; that he is of medieval or post-medieval origin; and lastly, that he is significant irrespective of age. Tim Darvill, Ronald Hutton and Barbara Bender acted as advocates for the three arguments. In addition to their own pleas they had each invited

several expert witnesses to strengthen their cases. A panel of assessors steered the inquiry and co-ordinated cross-examination and third-party questioning of the witnesses. The audience functioned as the jury and finally voted with a large majority in favour of the case for a prehistoric Romano-British origin.

Many archaeological TV documentaries, for example those on *Discovery Channel* including *Time Team*, tend to adopt detective-style narratives to tell their stories (see chapter 3). The same is true for a large number of adventure and computer games such as *Riddle of the Sphinx* (2000) and *The Mystery of the Mummy* (2003) (Felder et al 2003: 171-3; Schadla-Hall and Morris 2003). Even an entire museum exhibition has now been designed as a detective story. Exhibition maker and archaeologist Heidrun Derks (2003) created the fictitious detective Stahnke who accompanies visitors through the new exhibition about the Battle of Varus in Kalkriese in northwest Germany. Based on the notion of a search for clues, Stahnke explains to the visitor the various "criminalistic" methods by which archaeologists have been investigating the site of the battle. Children's literature and cartoons too, play on the notion of the archaeologist who, after digging up things, has to reconstruct what they were. The best-known example of this genre are Calvin and Hobbes' excavations. It is also the theme of Carin and Stina Wirsén's picture book *Rut & Knut go digging* (*Rut & Knut gräver ut*, 2000), where the two heroes find all sorts of bones and artefacts, eventually using them all to build a pirate ship.

The entire genre of the archaeologist as detective has often been parodied. If, as Warwick Bray (1981: 222) suggested, the intellectual health of a discipline can be measured by the parodies it generates, then archaeology is very healthy indeed. One brilliant example is the German satirist Hans Traxler's (1983) bestselling story of how the fairy tale archaeologist Georg Ossegg is gradually discovering, through various material clues and excavations, the historical truth behind the Grimm Brother's story of Hansel and Gretel. No less brilliant is the author and illustrator David Macaulay's (1979) account of the *Motel of the Mysteries*, a late twentieth century ruin re-discovered in 4022 by the mediocre amateur archaeologist Howard Carson. The site was to reveal "wonderful things" indeed about a mysterious lost civilization... Hilarious fun about current variations of the historical detective in TV documentaries specifically was made by Marcus Brigstocke in his own spoof series *We are History* (2000-1) (see chapter 2).

Arguably, a special case within the detective category is the antiquarian scholar, usually an elderly male professor with glasses and a beard, somewhat dull but not always

OLD POTS £1

unattractive, obsessed with his research — which he perceives as a large puzzle, keeping a journal containing his theories and a little out of this world. This was the role played by archaeologist Mortimer Wheeler on British TV during the 1950s (Jordan 1981; Russell 2002b: 43). Even the very popular figure of the excavating Swedish King Gustav VI Adolf (1882-1973) may fall into this category, although this should by no means be taken to denigrate his genuine interest (see Lagerqvist and Odelberg 1972).

The gentleman-like scholar, like the detective, creates light where there was darkness, solving academic mysteries through the skills of careful observation, pain-staking analysis, enormous knowledge, strict logic and some intuition when it matters most. In a way this character is thus a hero too, although not in the sense of the classical adventure discussed earlier (which is why some prefer to speak of an anti-hero in this context). The narrative that goes with scholarship, as seen in popular culture, bears nevertheless an astonishing resemblance to that common in adventures: scholars leave behind their own familiar world, fully committed to command other worlds; they work in their fields exploring uncharted territories without fear or hesitation; they make sensational discoveries and eventually they announce their enlightenment to the world at large, which in turn rewards them with recognition, although their own motivation is entirely selfless. Indiana Jones's father Professor Henry Jones, played by Sean Connery in *Indiana Jones and the Last Crusade*, is designed precisely in this mould. He does not like being disturbed and never had time for his son since he followed his personal quest of scholarship for all his life. Yet then the scholarly passion of his father suddenly merges with Indy's adventure and the professor's scholarship becomes as important as Indy's fighting skills for the successful completion of their joint adventure. In this case as well as in *The Mummy* and *Stargate* movies/TV series, the *Relic Hunter* films, the Lego *Adventurer* products and the *Doc Savage* series, among others, the detective/scholar and the adventurer together form the classic team for solving archaeological mysteries.

An added dimension to the scholarly detective is often that there are two or more of them competing with each other. As Neal Ascherson (2004: 152) put it, when these "bearded giants of the intellect" meet, the scholar is transformed into an "academic street fighter" hitting out at the other, so that "one professor's victory [becomes] the shattering defeat and discrediting of another." That kind of dynamic is also prominent in the compelling "fact-based" novels in which Ceram (1980 [1949]) and several others after him told the history of important archaeological discoveries. Although alternative archaeologists used to redefine such controversies in terms of orthodox establishment versus underdog

78

maverick, now even their proponents of mutually exclusive theories have taken to high-profile controversies from which both sides hope to emerge victorious (Picknett and Prince 2003: 186-9).

Throughout popular culture archaeology deals with mysteries where many pieces of a puzzle have to be found and then put together by the respective experts. Only at the end, the full picture will be revealed. Every discovery story is thus also a little detective story — and that is true for accounts of both academic and alternative archaeological research.

Detective story	Fact-based archaeological novel (Ceram)
1. The detective	1. The archaeologist
2. The crime, lying in the dark	2. The archaeological artefact, lying in the dark
3. The motive which can explain the crime	3. The key which can explain the artefact (e.g. Rosetta Stone)
4. Techniques of delay (false tracks, resistance, competition, envious opponents)	
5. Great excitement immediately before the revelation or discovery	

Similarities between the detective story and the fact-based archaeological novel as represented by Ceram. Source: Schörken (1995: 74). My translation.

These correspondences between criminological and archaeological mysteries are certainly one reason why archaeologists and archaeology occur frequently in detective fiction. Agatha Christie, whose Hercule Poirot is explicitly inspired by archaeological methodology, was also married to the archaeologist Max Mallowan and participated in a series of his excavations herself (Trümpler 2001). She saw archaeology as a puzzle about the past and mentioned in conversations that there were obvious parallels between the work of archaeologists and that of detectives (Joan Oates, pers. comm. 2002). Many other writers have seen these similarities too. The popular Swedish author Jan Mårtenson (*Caesars örn*, 1996), for instance, described in parallel the investigations of hobby detective Johan Homan and those of a team of archaeologists on Gotland. British examples that come

to mind are Ellis Peters' account of a series of mysterious discoveries at the imaginary Roman site of Aurae Phiala (*City of Gold and Shadows*, 1973) and Mike Ripley's crime novel about Angel encountering not only a shambolic archaeological dig but also an eccentric sponsor keen to dig into his own past (*Angel Underground*, 2002). The best-selling author Tony Hillerman (e.g. *A Thief of Time*, 1989) in turn likes to combine themes about native American archaeology with the work of his police officer Joe Leaphorn.

Vice versa, some archaeologists like Stanley Casson (*Murder by Burial*, 1938), Glyn Daniel (aka Dilwyn Rees, e.g. *The Cambridge Murders*, 1945), Barbara Mertz (aka Elizabeth Peters, numerous Amelia Peabody novels) and Gordon Willey (e.g. *Selena*, 1997) have also written detective novels themselves, usually featuring archaeologists. The American archaeologist and author Beverly Connor maintains a comprehensive website[36] contextualising her novels about the forensic anthropologist Diane Fallon resp. the Southeastern archaeologist Lindsay Chamberlain, who is "unfortunately accustomed to murder on archaeological sites" (from her online mystery *The Case of the Murdered Archaeologist*).

Detective/scholar archaeologists of popular culture:		
Dr. Cornelius	A chimpanzee in the film *The Planet of the Apes*	www.movieprop.com/ tvandmovie/PlanetoftheApes
Daniel Jackson, Egyptologist	The hero in the film *Stargate* and subsequent TV series *Stargate SG-1*	www.geocities.com/ eventmovies/stargate.htm; www.stargatesg1.com
Professor Henry Jones	Indiana Jones' father (see above)	www.theindyexperience.com; www.indianajones.com
Professor Kilroy, Professor Articus, Dr Charles Lightning	A character with different names in the Lego *Adventurers* theme featuring Johnny Thunder	www.geocities.com/ EnchantedForest/ Cottage/5900/Adventurers. html

---

36 http://www.athens.net/~bconnor

Martin Mystère	The hero in an Italian comic series	www.bvzm.com
Dr Eric Leidner	The murderer in Agatha Christie's *Murder in Mesopotamia* (1936)	www.agathachristie.com
Professor William Harper Littlejohn	A character in the 1930/40s *Doc Savage* novels by Lester Dent and other (associated comics, radio shows and a movie from 1975)	members.aol.com/the86floor; members.netvalue.net/robsmalley
Evelyn O'Connell (Carnarvon), Egyptologist	Major character in the *Mummy* films and recent role playing games	www.themummy.com
Amelia Peabody and Radcliff Emerson, Egyptologists	Main characters in a series of novels by Elizabeth Peters	www.mpmbooks.com/amelia
Jean-Luc Picard, Professor Richard Galen	The captain of the Enterprise and his former teacher in the TV series *Star Trek*	www.startrek.com
Professor Hercules Taragon, Americanist	A character in two *Tintin* adventures	www.tintin.com

However, in popular culture, not all archaeological scholars are successful detectives, becoming heroes in their own fields. Some seem to be doing little else than conducting arcane research through which they accumulate obscure facts and artefacts. They are from educated middle-class backgrounds and come across as dull and boring people, so that popular culture occasionally makes fun of them (Membury 2002: 11; Russell 2002b: 39). This, for example, is the case with Jean-Luc Picard, Captain of the *Enterprise* and a dedicated amateur archaeologist. When, in the *Star Trek* episode *Qpid*, he addressed

the Federation's Archaeology Council, his "scientific" speech is described (and indeed performed) as "dull" and "pedantic". Another boring archaeologist was depicted in the extremely popular 1980s BBC sitcom *Hi-De-Hi*, written by David Croft and Jimmy Perry. The series was set in a typical British holiday camp in the 1950s and 1960s. Jeffrey Fairbrother, a former professor of archaeology, is the awkward and uncomfortable new entertainment manager who introduces himself with the following words:[37]

> "I left my seat at Cambridge as Professor of Archaeology, essentially, to discover just how to stop being boring. It's no secret that being boring is what led to the end of my marriage, and I found, to my surprise, that many of my students were falling asleep during my lectures too because they were bored as well."

A similar character is Professor Roland Crump, the "distinguished archaeologist" in the British comedy *Carry On Behind* (1975). He is an uptight, confused and wimpish scholar who encounters numerous situations of sexual innuendo while excavating a Roman brothel with a mosaic depicting erotic scenes. Significantly, we meet him first while giving a lecture entitled "Getting to the bottom of things". Similarly bizarre characters are Ansgar and Loke who feature regularly in the Danish TV comedy series Wulff & Morgenthaler.[38] These two archaeologists are forever digging the same site, wear anoraks, sport bad hair cuts and talk a lot about women and sex.

All in all, scholars, like detectives, are widely considered benevolent and harmless. Indeed, their scholarship is often seen as appealing and enviable, although it may occasionally have its funny aspects too. In the context of the scholars' own families, however, the complete dedication given to their research can be more sad than funny. This is well illustrated by Henry Jones who, in *Indiana Jones and the Last Crusade*, emerges as a father who had been obsessed with scholarship for all his life and never had time for his son. At the end of the film he finally seems to realise his mistake (Son: "What did you find, Dad?" – Father: "Me?"). Similarly, when Sir Noel Cunliffe, the famous Oxford archaeologist in Julian Mitchell's play *Half-Life* (1977: 53), now retired, comes to reconsider his life he is forced to admit: "I've been buried all my life. I'm trying to scrape my way up to light and air." He learns (p. 57) that his institution, too, has to carry some of the blame: "Oxford's well known to protect people from reality. A great preserver of self-delusions."

---

37 http://www.geocities.com/TelevisionCity/Set/8261/fairbro.htm
38 http://www.dr.dk/wulffmorgenthaler

In addition, there can be a side to this character yet more worrying. Whether by some historical coincidence or as a result of misguided ambitions, the scholar may end up on the 'wrong' moral side. Such figures can become potent enemies even to their own colleagues, as demonstrated by the Nazi archaeologist Dr Elsa Schneider in *Indiana Jones and the Last Crusade* (1989) and the corrupt archaeologist Alex West who works for an auction house, in *Lara Croft:Tomb Raider* (2001).

> "All of scientific research into prehistory is a sort of jigsaw-puzzle. Fitting facts to theories until the sum of all the facts establishes without doubt a complete and irrefutable picture."
>
> Hammond Innes (1973: 241-2)

In another way scholarship can be dangerous too. Referral to scholarship in tricky questions always implies that – provided all the facts are known – there will be a single correct answer. Just as with the jigsaw puzzle, the skilled expert will first assemble all the pieces and then carefully fit them altogether until the complete image becomes visible. This is how archaeologists, so often, are presented in popular culture. Incidentally, this is also how archaeologists themselves like to see themselves, describing the process of their research by using detective metaphors. As reassuring as this view of the archaeologist may be, both for archaeologists and others, it is also misleading. In Rolf Jensen's terms (see chapter 1), the idea of the gradual completion of a puzzle may create "peace of mind" for everybody involved, but the complexities of life are often such that the notion of a single solution to complex issues appears to be naive at best. In puzzle terms, there will be far too many pieces than one can handle, far too few that actually fit with each other and many that will fit into one and the same places – and nowhere else. Often, a combination of different, partial answers based on local knowledge rather than universal scholarship, can in fact do better justice to competing perspectives.

Moreover, the notion of the scholar implies that their "cases" can be and need to be resolved by referring to outside expertise. Yet in practice it is often less than clear what kind of expertise would actually be required, who may be possessing it, to whom the experts themselves are accountable and in what way they can be controlled by those using their services. Such concerns have led to calls for a stronger democratisation of the sciences (see chapter 6).

An added problem arises when the role of archaeologist is effectively reduced to that of the scholarly expert and a simultaneous role as an independent thinker is made impossible. As the British archaeologist Yannis Hamilakis (2003: 108) reminded us in

the aftermath of the war against Iraq:

"we should reject the role of the professional specialist who provides expertise in their narrow field but who fails to question the meta-narratives and practices of nationalism, neo-colonialism and imperialism, within which this knowledge is deployed."

The R theme: the archaeologist making profound revelations

A third common stereotype of archaeology is that it is a source of sensational revelations, although they occur also in association with other sciences, especially the life sciences. Curiously, this theme has previously attracted little attention although it occurs frequently and is, as in the case of the other themes, easily recognisable. Not unusual, for example, are archaeological newspaper stories with headlines like "Dresden Stonehenge discovered: Stone Age observatory is 7000 years old!" (*Bildzeitung Dresden*, 7 August 2002; see p. 48), "Norrbotten was multi-cultural already 10,000 years ago" (*Norrländska Socialdemokraten*, 19 September 2003) or "Göteborg's inhabitants are really Germans" (*Aftonbladet*, 19 October 2002; all my translations). Examples for these kinds of revelations cannot always be blamed on 'sloppy' journalism but they are, at least in parts, the doing of archaeologists and scientists of other disciplines themselves:

"As science relies more and more upon legitimisation by the public, via the media, [...] science itself takes up the media's [...] habits, portraying the world as a place caught between salvation and catastrophe, breakthrough and flop: a sphere in which heroic scientists struggle to offer us, the public, longer life and greater well-being..." (Hargreaves and Ferguson 2000: chapter 2)

It has become normal to expect from archaeologists new revelations whenever they present their work (directly or via mediators) to large audiences. The stronger and more sensational the claim, the more "interesting" and "worthwhile" a specific project can be perceived to be. Parodies have made that principle particular obvious. For example, in 1999 the American satirical paper *The Onion* ran a story entitled "Archaeological Dig Uncovers Ancient Race of Skeleton People". After finding ancient skeletons, the excavator is cited as stating that "the implications are staggering...We now know that the skeletons we see in horror films and on Halloween are not mere products of the imagination, but actually lived on Earth. [...] These skeletons may, in fact, be ancestors to us all. Any of us could be part skeleton." [39] By the same token, on 1 April 2004, the campaign for awarding the German town of Bremen the title of "European Cultural Capital 2010" put out a short film and press statement announcing the "archaeological sensation" that the "mystery of the Sphinx of Gizeh" has been "revealed": it is said to have been part of a sculpture of the town musicians of Bremen, a well-known German fairy tale.[40]

Generally the R theme is compatible with both the A theme and the D theme and usually occurs in conjunction with either one or both of them. The basic notion is that at the end of an adventure or a detective story a sensational discovery is made that often contains a truth significant and important to everybody. In this vein, the British TV series *Time Team* promises that each programme "unlocks the secrets of the past in just three days" (after Cleere 2000: 91). The unrivalled master of this genre is the impressive Time Life book series on lost civilizations promising again and again to "explore ancient mysteries and unravel the secrets of lives once lived in..." (brochure slogan from 1998). How significant such "secrets" can be, is illustrated in Hammond Innes' adventure novel *Levkas Man* (1973). Here, a series of excavations and finds gradually reveal to a desperate palaeo-anthropologist that "Man is a killer" who "carries the seed of his own destruction in him", thus questioning whether there is "any hope for our species" (p. 260). Similarly large issues have been addressed in popular non-fiction literature about archaeology.

The German TV author Gisela Graichen (1995: 14, 22) suggested in one of the books accompanying her programmes that archaeologists could find the mechanisms that govern the rise and fall of civilizations and reveal the reasons why some societies flourish and others collapse. Based on their understanding of the past, archaeologists may thus be able to develop strategies of survival for our future as human beings. That motivation was shared by the Americans archaeologist Charles Redman and environmental historian

---

[39] http://www.theonion.com/content/node/29976
[40] Now available at http://web.archive.org/web/20050218012452/http://www.bremen2010.de/sixcms/detail.php?id=367

Jared Diamond. Hoping for "Lessons from a prehistoric 'Eden'" (the title of his first chapter), Redman studied the diversity of human environmental impacts which he considered a topic "that has direct relevance to the survival of modern society" (1999: 6). Similarly, Diamond contemplated in his best-selling book entitled *Collapse: How Societies Choose to Fail or Succeed* (2005) the ruins of vanished civilizations, asking whether our society too is in for a collapse and what we may be able to do about it given our knowledge about the past. The Swedish archaeologist Göran Burenhult (e.g. 1986: 10) made also much of the possibility to learn from primitive societies in order to cope better with future challenges to humanity's ambitions to survive.

In an illuminating study of archaeological non-fiction literature, including both "fringe" and "orthodox" books, the Canadian anthropologist Kathryn Denning (1999) showed that in quite a few of them the study of ancient civilizations led to warnings of some kind of apocalypse threatening our own society. Fortunately, the same studies also revealed "ancient wisdoms" which can help humanity to avoid the cataclysm (see also Picknett and Prince 2003: 177-8). It did not seem to make a principal difference in this respect whether the authors were 'good' academics like Paul Bahn and John Flenley or 'alternative' researchers like Robert Bauval and Graham Hancock. It is only a small step from here to the heroic Lara Croft whose archaeological expertise helps her directly to save the world from its imminent destruction by evil enemies. The archaeologist thus often comes across as a potential saviour, sometimes resembling a seer or messiah, whose revelations enlighten our ordinary lives and may even be able to save us from imminent doom. Although professional archaeologists may indeed occasionally entertain high hopes for the significance of their research, it is uncertain whether they will really be able to help human survival on planet Earth.

> "We've got to track it, go to it, investigate it. This is the ultimate artifact, Leonore. Think. A device that challenges the basic parameters of the universe itself. What race designed it? Why?" [p. 383]
>
> Inter-galactic archaeologist Michael Ralston realised to his horror that he was discovering the future, no longer just unearthing the past. He had to track down the devastating chaos field and stop it wreaking total havoc throughout the universe. The trail of catastrophe stretched back into deep space – and was moving forward into our own galaxy. [Back cover blurb]
>
> From Robert Vardeman's sci-fi novel *Weapons of Chaos* (omnibus edition, 1989)

The reason why archaeologists should have special access to such great truths goes beyond their ability to solve mysteries and recover treasures. The American archaeologist John Fritz (1973: 76) emphasized that the archaeologist is "an intermediary between the worldly and the other worldly and between the quick and the dead." In as much as it is possible to bring lost civilizations and the dead back to life and make ancient artefacts speak, terms often used

to describe archaeology, it involves supernatural powers and achieves true miracles. As Fritz (1973: 77-8) went on to explain, "to watch archeological techniques is to watch the archeologist use his [or her] power to deal with the power of the past" and "to learn about the past from archeologists is to be enlightened about the nature of another world".

Nowhere is the notion of the archaeologist having access to eternal truths better exemplified than in the *Indiana Jones* film scripts. Whereas in *Raiders of the Lost Ark*, Indiana Jones seeks to recover the Ark of the Covenant, which is believed still to hold the Ten Commandments, in the *Last Crusade* he hunts, together with his father, for nothing less than the Holy Grail. Archaeology thus harbours natural links to the supernatural. In other contexts, similar links emerge between archaeology and the world of ancient wisdoms and primitive ways of life that can show us ways to salvation (Steuben 1977: 13-4). Here is the link between archaeology and esoteric knowledge that also explains why the astrologer Jonathan Cainer's shop in York sells books about ancient civilizations and their monuments (see chapter 2).

Erich von Däniken-style archaeology[41]

The Swiss best-seller author Erich von Däniken (born 1935) made his fame by revealing the possibility of extra-terrestrial origins of ancient human civilizations. Däniken (who incidentally never claimed to be an archaeologist) has been a master of linking archaeological "mysteries", such as European megaliths, Egyptian pyramids, Maya pyramids in Mesoamerica and the Nazca lines in Peru, with large existential questions about humans in the universe. Taking the R theme to an extreme, he points to possible explanations involving visits by advanced beings from outer space. Although his account lacks plausibility, Däniken is a master at evoking possibilities that many people find intriguing. He wonders, for instance, whether Stonehenge might contain "a message for the future of humanity" and whether that message may be waiting for us on a certain asteroid far away in the universe which the monument might be pointing to. But even Däniken does not claim certainty. Instead, he suspects rather suggestively that "we have been missing something important" about Stonehenge.... (Däniken and Däniken 2005: 72, my translation).

Däniken's A.A.S.R.A. (Archaeology, Astronautics and SETI Research Association) is trying to substantiate his "Paleo-SETI theory" that extraterrestrials have visited Earth in ancient times. Questions that are explicitly addressed include the following:

- did extraterrestrial visitors interfere with or even guide human and cultural evolution?

- what are the implications and consequences of proving "We are not alone – and never have been"?

- are we really the pinnacle of creation?

Now Däniken has built *Mystery Park*, a theme park about his speculations and the best-known case studies of his argument (Däniken and Däniken 2005). The park in the Swiss town of Interlaken opened in May 2003. The skilful presentation of some of the largest archaeological "mysteries" of the world and Däniken's suggestive answers attracted more than 330,000 visitors in the first seven months. *Mystery Park* also won the Swiss Tourism Award 2003. What is more, with over 65 million sold books, Däniken alone has probably reached more readers than all the writings of professional archaeologists worldwide put together. Now he plans a science-fiction TV series "Chariots of the Gods" in a format resembling the *X Files*.

As always, "all ends with question marks"... (Däniken and Däniken 2005: 77, my translation)

When a certain threshold of revealing secrets is overstepped there is, however, the risk that the past takes revenge. As *The Mummy* films and numerous novels and adventure games vividly illustrate, the unscrupulous archaeologist who disturbs the peace of the

---

[41] see http://www.daniken.com; http://www.legendarytimes.com; http://www.mysterypark.ch

dead and compulsively seeks to recover secrets of ancient civilizations may have to face the mighty forces guarding them. That holds in Egypt as much as in the south-western United States (e.g. Presfton and Child 1999). Archaeologists run the risk of

> "tampering with forces that they do not understand. They are the people who raid the tomb, irrespective of the wishes and warnings of the local or indigenous population, awaken the dead, activate the curse, and bring down some immense supernatural nasty upon the world." (Russell 2002b: 46)

89

It is not surprising that this metaphysical dimension of archaeology enjoys considerable public interest. On the one hand, archaeology commands some of the same appeal as horror movies or the *X Files*. For all of them hold that when you are dealing with unknown mysteries, you can expect some nasty surprises. Steuben (1977: 14) was probably correct in assuming that the interest in archaeology is often of the same kind as the interest in flying saucers.

On the other hand, the archaeologist addresses several of the same large, existential questions which also account for peoples' interest in matters surrounding death, human nature and predictions for the future. For an archaeologist, it is easily possible to provide historical perspectives on ideas about life after death, to speculate about what is and is not changing in the way humans behave, or to suggest social, cultural or environmental developments that might continue in the future. Even though satisfying the public demand in addressing these issues is arguably an important social function of archaeology and cultural heritage (Burström 2004), archaeologists are however often reluctant to get into any kind of further speculations that cannot withstand scientific scrutiny. "Alternative" archaeologists like Erich von Däniken or Graham Hancock have been able to claim the vacated territory with considerable success, enjoying much attention. An additional, regular selling point they have championed is the claim that academics are conspiring to hold back inevitable conclusions of research, since the revelations would threaten established paradigms.

A recent survey in the UK (English Heritage 2000) concluded that people will increasingly be looking to the heritage sector "to help provide continuity, relevance, and meaning in their everyday lives". Professional archaeologists should keep this in mind. But the most important aspect of the R theme is not that archaeologists might *really* have access to other-worldly truths which others do not. As the regular appearance of the R theme in popular archaeology shows, people are interested and attentive as soon as archaeologists are *trying* to answer some of the Big Questions of the Universe. Moreover, they are even willing to suspend disbelief when archaeologists occasionally come up with some really Big Answers. Significantly, a common characterisation of the more outlandish claims by Erich von Däniken or Graham Hancock is that "it's just a theory, *like all the others*." For many, their spectacular suggestions evidently do not appear to be different *in kind* to any "other" archaeological theory and are worth considering to the same extent. Hancock himself is well aware of what it takes to catch the public imagination:

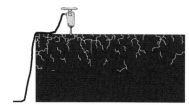

"What galvanises public attention are those new insights or evidence that make it reasonable to consider the possibility that a radical, alternative interpretation of history might, against all the odds, be correct." (Graham Hancock, e-mail communication 2006)

This example shows that unlike many religious missionaries, archaeologists – and others investigating archaeological sites – generally command trust and will be listened to when they announce new results of their research. The "revelatory might of archaeology" (Denning 1999: 101) gives the archaeologist a particular responsibility to consider carefully what is being 'revealed'. At the same time, that particular brand attribute is an enormous possibility, since we can be confident that when archaeologists seek to break out of the straightjacket of scientific caution they are likely to find some very attentive audiences.

The C theme: the archaeologist taking care of ancient sites and finds

A final theme within which archaeology is being given meaning in contemporary popular culture has only over the past few years gained in significance, as developer-funded rescue archaeology and cultural heritage management have been thoroughly transforming the landscape of professional archaeology throughout Europe and beyond. Archaeologists have become the Heritage Police (Welinder 2000: 86-7).

This theme revolves around the notion that in managing ancient sites and finds, archaeologists bear the responsibility of taking care of what are scarce and non-renewable resources (Holtorf 2005: chapter 8). Accordingly, the archaeologist, whether a civil servant or an employee of a commercial company, is a caring specialist with limited time and limited resources who tries to salvage, for the benefit of society and humankind, valuable archaeological sites or artefacts – and the historical information they may possess – from decay or destruction. In addition, these professional rescuers, who are committed to working according to ethical principles, also fight things like tomb-raiding (as does Lara Croft) and the illicit antiquities trade. Incidentally, such elements are also central in how archaeologists see themselves (Welinder 2000). That is reflected, for example, in information signs that explain to the public why there is nothing to see of the rock art for which they came to Aspeberget, part of the World Heritage site of Tanum in Bohuslän, Sweden: the archaeologists cared so much for their sites that in order to protect some of the finest art from further weathering and erosion, they covered it up with soil (Gustafsson and Karlsson 2004: 126-7).

Whereas the A theme is usually far-away archaeology, the C theme tends to be close-to-home archaeology. The former can be appreciated in national and indeed international media, but the latter is particularly visible in local media such as newspapers. Local papers contain numerous reports about precisely what has been rescued where and which preserved archaeological sites or recovered finds exhibited in museums might draw visitors to the area. So strong is this fascination with caring for ancient sites and preserving historical evidence at risk that local rescue projects might even then be deemed newsworthy when nothing has been found: "No archaeological finds where National Road 29 will run" (*Blekinge Läns Tidning*, 2 October 2002, my translation).

The C theme is now also entering the worlds of film and fiction. Joe Pachinko's underground novel *Swamp!* is a timely account of a few archaeologists working under harsh conditions for a somewhat absurd commercial company. These archaeologists have learned their

lessons: "It's not just an adventure, it's a job" (Pachinko 1997: 197). And that job is pretty bizarre:

> "Contract archaeology companies are paid NOT to find anything. If they do accidentally find something, the faster they can dig it up, the less they have to pay the field crew and the more money they can make. Therefore, it is in the contract archaeologists' best interest not to find anything. Of course sometimes they can't help it and find something anyway. It's upsetting but that's showbiz." (Pachinko 1997: 99-100).

That genre is growing fast. The well-known Swedish author P. C. Jersild published in 2003 a novel (*De ondas kloster*) about a small archaeological rescue firm struggling under various pressures as clues about the medieval site under investigation emerge. Similarly, in Deborah Cannon's thriller *The Raven's Pool* (2004), the archaeologists are getting embroiled in a battle with a ruthless developer who could not care less about an important ancient site... In the Hollywood movie *The Body* (2001), a rescue dig in Jerusalem brings to light nothing less than the remains of Christ. Film archaeologist Dr Sharon Golban explains the circumstances of the discovery in a way that Indiana Jones, his father, or Erich von Däniken would hardly have chosen: "They wanted to put up flats in about three months so we had to be quick." The *National Geographic Society*, too, is now extending the appeal of their documentaries to include the C theme. A DVD I bought of the 2002 production *Inca Mummies: Secrets of a Lost Empire* features on its cover not only some of the usual emblems of the A theme but also an invitation to "join archaeologists racing to rescue priceless Inca relics from looters and urban sprawl."

The C and D themes are very compatible with each other and indeed often combined. Among my previous examples only Pachinko's novel is better associated with the A theme. The C and D themes are nevertheless by no means interchangeable. The archaeologist as specialist caretaker in a commercial urban world is more likely than any other archaeologist to work at home rather than abroad. Also, he or she is not a detective carrying a notebook and a magnifying glass but rather a professional expert who wears either suit and tie or protective clothing suggested by the appropriate Health and Safety regulations (see below).

Even science-fiction adventures, which always had a leaning towards featuring archaeologists, have begun to reflect these real changes to the discipline on planet

Earth (Russell 2002a). For example, the *Star Trek* episode *Q-less* (1993) featuring rogue archaeologist Vash, who has previously been expelled from the Federation's Archaeology Council for selling illicit artefacts, contains a strong ethical message. When she is resuming her illegal activities, omnipotent alien Q informs the bridge crew of space station *Deep Space Nine* that Vash is "setting Federation ethics back two hundred years. Believe me, gang, she is far more dangerous to you than I am." Similarly, the sci-fi novel *The Ship Who Searched* (McCaffrey and Lackey 1992) makes much of professional archaeological ethics vis-à-vis ruthless looters and artefact smugglers that abound in the universe.

One of my favourite archaeological sci-fi novels is Jack McDevitt's *Deepsix* (2001) in which an archaeological team finds itself in a scenario where a rogue moon hurtling through space is about to obliterate the last opportunity to study a rare planet with ancient remains. As the back cover explains, the group must "glean whatever they can about its life forms and lost civilizations before time runs out." As much as this is also an adventure story, the particular kind of threat the archaeologists face is one that Indiana Jones would find extremely foreign to the same extent to which it would be extremely familiar to any professional archaeologist of our time. The same can be said about the particular challenges waiting for players in Channel 4's online archaeological whodunnit "Time Detectives":

> "A local developer wants to build a housing estate on the quiet rural fields of Teamchester. You and your team of specialists have been called in to do an archaeological assessment of the area. You have just three days to discover the lost story of the Teamchester fields. If you can't come up with a conclusive report at the end of the last day the developers will move in."[42]

The C theme in archaeology has both comical and tragic elements. On the one hand, precisely why should anybody want to rescue a few ancient artefacts? On the other hand, the archaeologist can often not prevent but only alleviate the destruction of archaeological sites. In films like the Swedish comedy *Den ofrivillige golfaren* (1991), where a somewhat hopeless character played by Claes Månsson represents the county archaeologist Berglund, both elements are coming together. The audience smiles about the seemingly ridiculous endeavours of the naive and inept archaeologist but at the same time feels for this poor guy who is trying to do his important job without being

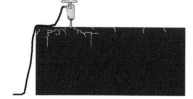

---

[42] http://www.channel4.com/history/timeteam/game.html

taken seriously by anybody. Significantly, when I began my project, many of my new Swedish colleagues suggested that this is the film I ought to watch... No doubt they were recognizing one part of themselves in the figure of Berglund.

The work of the caretaker archaeologist is usually appreciated by people. For example, in the digital strategy game *Tropico: Paradise Island* (2002) you are installed as the new dictator on an imaginary Caribbean island and have to develop your country. Among the many options you have, professional archaeologists can be employed in order to create and maintain tourist sites which will benefit your economy (Felder et al 2003: 174). But when personal interests are involved, e.g. when peoples' personal beliefs, finances or livelihoods are concerned, the stakes rise quickly and the archaeologist can be perceived as a formidable enemy. It may suddenly appear questionable why all this academic attention to ancient remains should be so sensible after all.

For example, in the events following the discovery of *Seahenge* on the Norfolk coast in England, various New Age and pagan groups as well as local supporters presented themselves as the true protectors of this magic site, whereas the archaeologists who were trying to 'rescue' it from destruction came across in the mass media as desecrators and violators of these people's legitimate interests (Ascherson 2004: 147).

Very different circumstances are described in the British film *Pascali's Island* (1988). Set on an Aegean island during the end of the Ottoman Empire the local Pasha feels threatened by the archaeologist Anthony Bowles who lets it be known that he will report his valuable discoveries to the national authorities in Constantinople so that the Sultan can take care of it in the proper way. The irony is that Bowles himself turns out to be a swindler who is seeking to get rich from the greedy Pasha.

The archaeologist's clothes

One way in which the different themes that govern the meaning of archaeology in popular culture become prominent is how archaeologists are dressed. After all, in the emerging *Experience Economy* it is important to avoid negative cues and ensure the integrity of the customer experience by role-appropriate clothing (Pine and Gilmore 1999: 55-6).

- "This week we will be looking at some more - er - archaeology thingies; but best of all there will be lots of close-up shots of my latest McQueen and Prado, tight, but durable outdoor range."

The adventure hero dresses in colonial style, often resembling camping gear. As Michael French (n.d.) put it, "if Indiana Jones' khaki and leather outfit is in line with the outdoors wear of the 1930s, which it is, then Lara's khaki shorts, boots, and spandex are the very definition of 1990s adventure wear." Key elements of that look are the sun protection – preferably the pith helmet, the "practical" shirt and trousers with many pockets, the solid boots and the earthen khaki-colours that all pieces have in common. The traditional archaeological adventure wear does not only evoke colonial times but also the great time of travelling at the turn of the last century and of course the more recent image of the *Camel* man (Stern and Tode 2002: 72). Today, if you want to create an archaeologist recognisable at first glance, this is the look you choose – as so many caricatures demonstrate (Russell 2002b: 49-50). Vice versa, if you create real colonial-style fashion, you will choose to shoot your photographs on an actual excavation, preferably in Egypt (see Holtorf 2005: fig. 3.1).

The scholar, on the other hand, wears jacket and tie or, better, a bow-tie. Not infrequently glasses and a beard adorn this character too, e.g. Professor Henry Jones. As Tom Stern

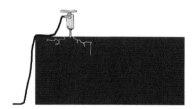

and Thomas Tode (2002: 72) observed, when in TV documentaries, name, title and institution are blended in just above the waist of archaeologists wearing such scholar wear, this does not clash but accentuates the appearance by emphasizing the charisma of authority that is already implied by the clothes anyway.

The field archaeologist is generally characterised by very different wear that is often deliberately unfashionable (Stern and Tode 2002: 77). *Time Team* presenter Tony Robinson once said that you could distinguish archaeologists by their poor dress and terrible haircuts. Mick

ARCHAEOLOGICUS ACADEMICUS PEDAGOGICUS

ARCHAEOLOGICUS ACADEMICUS EXCAVATOR

(THREATENED BY ***ARCHAEOLOGICUS COMMERCIALATIS CONSULTANTIS***)

WINTER PLUMAGE

SUMMER PLUMAGE

KNOW YOUR ARCHAEOLOGIST

Aston, one of the *Time Team* heroes, admitted that "we're complete scruffbags" and added, significantly, as many other archaeologists too could have said, "but I don't care. I'm not remotely interested in appearances, life's too short for that".[43]

Both archaeologists and people of the past found, or find, themselves in situations that are closer to nature and more 'primitive' than how we normally live today. In this sense, too, the archaeologist can appear to be "out of this world" (Stern and Tode 2002: 77). Fieldwork wear shows how properties (or stereotypes) of the period being investigated are being transferred onto the archaeologist. Colourful Viking personalities who experienced adventures and made discoveries, having to cope with the many challenges of their

---

[43] http://www.building-history.pwp.blueyonder.co.uk/Mick/Mick.htm

OLD POTS £1

lives and wearing Thor hammers around their necks, are being excavated by colourful archaeologists who are engaged in adventurous fieldwork making discoveries, having to cope with the many challenges of their excavations and wearing Thor hammers around their necks (Petersson 1994: 61, 70-1). For some, these convergences may even imply a privileged understanding of the past being investigated.

However, as recently stated on the *British Archaeological Jobs Resource* discussion group, "just because I don't choose to dress as a medieval peasant doesn't mean I can't understand the archaeology of a medieval site." However that may be, archaeologists in the field certainly tend to look odd and maybe even exotic in their all-weather gear or combat clothes, unshaven or only half-dressed (Petersson 1994: 39). This archaeological field fashion has been well captured in David Webb's photograph series "Diggers" showing real archaeologists on excavations.[44]

The same can certainly not be said for another kind of fashion that has come to be associated with field archaeology in recent years, as it became firmly associated with the C theme. Certainly in Sweden, archaeologists in the field now tend to wear protective gear in very bright colours that are designed akin to the clothes of workers employed on road construction or building sites. Such health-and-safety wear signifies the competent professional working in a professional environment. It also makes archaeologists highly visible in their role as the Heritage Police. In these clothes, the archaeologist is no longer exhibiting his dreams and aspirations (as the adventurer), his higher abilities (as the detective/scholar), or

---

[44] http://www.archdiggers.co.uk/diggers/

his own personality (as the generic field archaeologist) but his professional practice (as the specialist attending to a scarce resource). Out of the field, the same archaeologist appears in an odd-looking suit, as if somewhat out of place (e.g. county archaeologist Berglund in *Den ofrivilliga golfaren*).

Often, the styles are not pure but mixed. For example, *Time Team* star excavator Phil Harding, arguably on most occasions exhibits fieldwork wear, although I also remember having seen him wearing elements of health-and-safety wear. Stephanie Moser (forthcoming), an archaeologist specialising in representations, described him however as an adventurer:

> "With his long hair, leather jacket, jeans, hat and strong regional accent, this fieldworker lives up to the popular conception of what it means to be an archaeologist. The cowboy type hat that he wears is of particular significance as a symbol of adventure and exploration."

As this example illustrates, the same clothes can be interpreted in different ways. The statements being made through fashion are anything but harmless and irrelevant though. As the popularity of formal or informal uniforms in society shows, clothes are not trivial for the image that is conveyed about oneself and one's profession. Heated discussions can emerge among professionals about how one should, or should not, dress as an archaeologist. For example, when, in 1996, David Webb published some of his images in the British *Institute of Field Archaeology*'s newsletter, they created an animated discussion. Whereas some felt that they rang particularly true, others argued that the numerous breaches of Health and Safety regulations and poor living conditions shown reflected badly on the IFA and the "good practice" and professionalism they were trying to promote (Swain 1997).

This issue recently surfaced again in a discussion on the German discussion group *arch-de* (in February 2003). The arguments raged between those advocating a professional image of an archaeologist wearing appropriately "neat" clothes like "insurance reps or doctors" and others who were not prepared to give up their beloved army wear with many "practical" large pockets and other useful features (cf. Russell 2002b: 50). What some considered as "scruffy old stuff" (*schlampiges Räuberzivil*), signifying a desire to be different from the rest of society, were described as "comfortable" clothes in line with public expectations by others who in turn mocked those in suits as "tie idiots in

uniform" (*uniformierte Krawattenheinis*). The latter responded by insisting that only neat packaging in "middle-class outfits" can express the credibility of a respectable profession and thus lead to success in tough financial negotiations. A very similar and similarly heated, debate took place on the *British Archaeological Jobs Resource* discussion group one year later. Through the clothes the archaeologist wears, then, various messages are conveyed that all seem to relate back to one question that does not seem to be resolved in popular culture either: is archaeology a job for professionals or a life-style for particularly dedicated individuals?

These are issues somebody like John Walker, Chief Executive of the York Archaeological Trust, is well aware of. Although he wore a suit and tie when I met him, according to his own testimony, he comes from an archaeological sub-culture which he calls "the drunks" and which is distinct from another such sub-culture which he calls the "young managers". His maxim is that as archaeologists we need to use the widely held image of archaeology to our advantage. When meeting politicians, for example, it is not necessarily the best strategy to wear suit and tie in order to state that "I am one of you", since they are far better at dressing in this style anyway. In such circumstances Walker therefore prefers to wear what he calls "normal" clothes, since it gives him the advantage of coming across as "a little peculiar" and "the eccentric archaeologist", incorporating some of the stereotypes of archaeologists that abound in popular culture. A beard, he says, is necessary for that reason, too.

Alternative themes

Any categorisation has its limits in where it draws boundaries between different types and with reference to those types that do not fit in any of the categories. As to the former, my own four themes are certainly inter-linked in many ways, and I have pointed to some of these links at the appropriate places in the text. As to the latter, my own attempt at categorising the meanings of archaeology in popular culture has not been able to place convincingly a number of reoccurring depictions which I would like to mention at least briefly now. These are interesting portrayals for the reason that they do not fit into a scheme of fairly well-known stereotypes and they deserve a much closer study and explanation, though not in this book.

Monty Python's Flying Circus, Episode 21[45]

ANIMATION: *a sketch about an archaeological find leads to:*
CAPTION: "ARCHAEOLOGY TODAY"

Interview set for archaeology program. Chairman and two guests sit in chair in front of a blow-up of an old cracked pot.

Interviewer	Hello. On "Archaeology Today" tonight I have with me Professor Lucien Kastner of Oslo University.
Kastner	Good evening.
Interviewer	How tall are you, professor?
Kastner	... I beg your pardon?
Interviewer	How tall are you?
Kastner	I'm about five foot ten.
Interviewer	... and an expert in Egyptian tomb paintings. Sir Robert ... *(turning to Kastner)* are you really five foot ten?
Kastner	Yes.
Interviewer	Funny, you look much shorter than that to me. Are you slumped forward in your chair at all?
Kastner	No, er I...
Interviewer	Extraordinary. Sir Robert Eversley, who's just returned from the excavations in El Ara, and you must be well over six foot. Isn't that right, Sir Robert?
Sir Robert	*(puzzled)* Yes.
Interviewer	In fact, I think you're six foot five aren't you?
Sir Robert	Yes.
	Applause from off. Sir Robert looks up in amazement.
Interviewer	Oh, that's marvelous. I mean you're a totally different kind of specimen to Professor Kastner. Straight in your seat, erect, firm.
Sir Robert	Yes. I thought we were here to discuss archaeology.
Interviewer	Yes, yes, of course we are, yes, absolutely, you're absolutely right! That's positive thinking for you. *(to Kastner)* You wouldn't have said a thing like that, would you? You five-foot-ten weed. *(he turns his back very ostentatiously on Kastner)* Sir Robert Eversley, who's very interesting, what have you discovered in the excavations at El Ara?
Sir Robert	*(picking up a beautiful ancient vase)* Well basically we have found a complex of tombs...
Interviewer	Very good speaking voice.
Sir Robert	... which present dramatic evidence of Polynesian influence in Egypt in the third dynasty which is quite remarkable.
Interviewer	How tall were the Polynesians?
Kastner	They were...

---

[45] abbreviated from http://www.ibras.dk/montypython/episode21.htm

POTS
£1

Interviewer	Sh!
Sir Robert	Well, they were rather small, seafaring...
Interviewer	Short men, were they... eh? All squat and bent up?
Sir Robert	Well, I really don't know about that...
Interviewer	Who were the tall people?
Sir Robert	I'm afraid I don't know.
Interviewer	Who's that very tall tribe in Africa?
Sir Robert	Well, this is hardly archaeology.
Interviewer	The Watutsi! That's it – the Watutsi! Oh, that's the tribe, some of them were eight foot tall. Can you imagine that. Eight foot of Watutsi. Not one on another's shoulders, oh no – eight foot of solid Watutsi. That's what I call tall.
Sir Robert	Yes, but it's nothing to do with archaeology.
Interviewer	*(knocking Sir Robert's vase to the floor)* Oh to hell with archaeology!

There is for example the archaeologist as a "vulnerable romantic" (Solomon 1998). Although this character is arguably linked to the A theme and often, for example, wears similar clothes, the archaeologist Tom Baxter in the movie *The Purple Rose of Cairo* (1985) is no Indiana Jones, who would probably never describe himself as Baxter does: "I am honest, dependable, courageous, romantic and a great kisser". When this "poetic little archaeologist" falls in love with a woman he gives up his archaeological explorations, telling her "I want to learn about the real world with you."

Adventurous in a different way is the young French archaeologist Lina in the B-movie *Summer Lovers* (1982). While working on the excavation site of Akrotiri on Santorini, exciting Lina enters into a romantic relationship with a visiting American tourist and his girlfriend, both of whom are attracted to her. In this portrayal, the archaeologist represents the intriguing Other through whom the two Americans ultimately find to each other again.

Then there is the archaeologist as a fairly ordinary person in an ordinary social context, with all the ordinary problems that may entail but that have nothing to do with archaeology. The German author Barbara Frischmuth, for example, showed in her novel *Bindungen* (1980) how the archaeologist Fanny looks back at her family past and contemplates her present life while visiting her sister who has built up a seemingly happy family idyll. The German film *Liebe auf den ersten Blick* (Love at First Sight, 1991) tells the story of the archaeologist Zenon Bloch, who is a widower, unemployed, living off state benefit and a single father of two small children. He falls in love with the single mother

and futurologist Elsa. Other stories about the archaeologist as a lover and normal person are *The Archaeologist* (1998) by the academic Richard Jenkins and *The Realms of Gold* (1975) by the English writer Margaret Drabble. In the latter novel, the famous archaeologist Frances Wingate, divorced and mother of four, has escaped a past of marital violence. While she finds herself madly in love with the weird and married academic Karel Schmidt, she is in the process of re-discovering her family history. There are other examples for the archaeologist as an ordinary person too (see e.g. Stern and Tode 2002: 77-8).

The most striking variation of this theme can be found in Japanese Anime and Manga which frequently feature archaeologists that are depicted as "nice, forgetful and well-meaning males, usually young" (Douglas Watt, e-mail correspondence 2004). In *Cardcaptor Sakura* there is, for example, the archaeologist Fujitaka Kinomoto (aka Aiden Avalon) who is a busy professor at the local university. Although he is often absent, Fujitaka is a loving father of two children including Sakura herself. Since his wife died at the age of 27 he raises them on his own. In all these cases, the main focus is on the non-professional family life of the archaeologist.

> "Japanese Anime treat the archaeologist like we treat a businessman or scientist in our movies and books. A father, who gets wrapped up in his work, is a bit scatterbrained and disorganized but loves his kids. There typically is not a mother figure, either she is dead or she is very ill. The father still loves her regardless though. Possibly he buries himself in his work to help forget the loneliness." (Renee Kennedy-Martin e-mail correspondence. 2004)

Conclusions

In this chapter I distinguished and discussed four main themes which can account for practically all meanings of archaeology in contemporary popular culture: the archaeologist as adventurer (A theme), as detective and scholar (D theme), as the source of profound revelations (R theme) and as caretaker of the remains of the past (C theme). Each theme represents one particular dimension of what has been called "archaeo-appeal" (Holtorf 2005: chapter 9). Significantly, there are some aspects that all these themes share:

None of the four themes take the past itself particularly seriously. Mostly, the archaeologist is portrayed not in relation to his actual ability to find out what happened in the past but in relation to certain qualities that are associated with this basic ambition. These qualities

may be the adventurous character of archaeological fieldwork, the exciting detective-work that leads to important discoveries which may solve historical mysteries, the possibility of eventually being able to make great revelations of wide significance and the professional duties of the specialist who takes good care of the archaeological heritage as a non-renewable resource. It is as if any specific historical information or indeed interpretation has only meaning in so far as it contributes to any of these themes, making the adventure more adventurous, the mystery more (or less) mysterious, the revelation more likely (or pertinent), or the protection more urgent.

In none of the four themes are the actual results of archaeological work particularly important. Instead, what matters most are various aspects of the process of doing archaeology (Daniel 1964: 162; Borbein 1981: 60; Holtorf 2004): the archaeologist's own heroic journey, the gradual piecing together of the case by locating and analysing significant clues, the constantly maintained hope that some true revelation will emerge from on-going work and the knowledge that scarce remains are being managed and treated responsibly. Just like an adventure story is not characterised by precisely what the hero accomplishes but how he gets there, so a detective story does not rely a lot on what the solution of the case eventually is and professional management of a scarce resource is not really about protection for any specific site or artefact and its historical information. I would argue that even great archaeological revelations are often more effective at making audiences gasp at *how* somebody could have reached them than at making them appreciate the validity of *what* they actually imply.

These observations are specific to the meaning of archaeology in contemporary Western popular culture. However, the phenomenon that the object and the results of scientific studies can seem less interesting than the desire and the process of studying themselves is not unique to archaeology. They occur also in many other sciences which feature unsolved mysteries, adventurous fieldwork, searches for evidence and the prospects of large revelations, among other popular themes. In other words, all scientific disciplines are to some extent perceived and appreciated in metaphorical terms (Haynes 1994; MacClancy 2005).

The implications of the conclusions of this and all previous chapters will be discussed in the final chapter, which will draw the book to a close. Before that I need to discuss though the principal models that can govern professional archaeologists' engagement with the meaning of their subject in popular culture.

Chapter 6

Strategies of engagement

The full title of the project of which this book is the outcome was "The portrayal of archaeology in contemporary popular culture – opportunity or obstacle for the promotion of cultural heritage?" Chapters 1 to 5 discussed different aspects of the first part of this agenda. This and the following chapter, in turn, will address the second part: that crucial question of what, if anything, archaeologists are to make of the way archaeology is portrayed in popular culture.

For many archaeologists the key issue in this context appears to be that they feel fundamentally misrepresented regarding the depiction of both the existing knowledge about the past and their own occupation. They would like to change the way archaeology is portrayed, to make it more accurate. Indeed, in some cases, unrealistic public expectations for archaeology are created that lead to disappointment when the professionals cannot meet those (Felder et al 2003: 162-3). The resulting frustrations on both sides are understandable, especially if you keep in mind the degree to which archaeologists are typically emotionally attached to their profession as well as to their subject. Complaints about misrepresentations in films and the mass media are therefore very common. The question is, however, whether it is not the archaeologists who in turn misunderstand the role and function of these media which are about perceptual rather than strictly referential realities, presenting dramatic rather than strictly veritable truths. In other words, "the audience's perceived reality is more important than the scientists' referential reality" (Frank 2003: 453).

> "a minor television production company approached my anthropology department, looking for a consultant [and I accepted the position]... At our first meeting, all the producer really wanted was an accurate picture of what a 'real' archaeological dig looked like. He wanted the dig site to look authentic, but within the bounds of his [and the audience's] *idea* of a dig site's appearance. This included lots of shovels and pith helmets, and local natives doing the digging work while the archaeologists watched; basically, a low-budget, scaled-down version of the excavation site from *Raiders of the Lost Ark*."
>
> Scott Frank (2003: 455)

Even when Hollywood uses science consultants, as is increasingly the case,

their task is not to ensure that films depict scientific realities but instead to help turning what is referentially unreal into something that *seems* real, thus improving the film's perceptual reality (Frank 2003). Often, archaeologists are not aware of this subtle distinction. The author and historian Neil Asher Silberman (1999: 82) doubted therefore that archaeology is ready for prime time:

> "Maybe it's time that members of the discipline [of archaeology] recognize that popularization is not merely repeating scholarly hypotheses in simple language so as to be understandable to the great unwashed."

Pointing out "archaeological flaws" in the Lara Croft films, for instance, is an undertaking that is entirely unnecessary (Rose 2003). Quite simply, such films do not mean to show how archaeologists really work. In his review of *Indiana Jones and the Last Crusade*, the archaeologist John Gowlett (1990: 157) warned accordingly against over-reactions by his colleagues:

> "I cannot think of anything worse than pontificating upon whether any archaeology in this fails to meet reality. That would be about as worthwhile as spotting the impossibilities of physics in *Star Wars*."

The overwhelming majority of people do not seem to have difficulties in distinguishing film realities from lived realities, past or present. I do not think that more than a very few believe that all professional archaeologists literally seek golden treasures in the jungle. But the most important point here is not the fact that professional archaeology and popular culture operate within very different frames of reference – separate discourses – that are widely recognised for what they are. Instead, it is crucial to step back from the immediate representations and realities and consider some of the bigger issues at stake on a broader social and political level. These issues are largely about the relations between science and society.

In the following I will be referring to three principal models for these relations between science and society. The underlying distinctions are modified from the work of Peter Healey (1999) and others who recently contributed to the discussions around what used to be called the "public understanding of science" (see e.g. Gregory and Miller 1998; House of Lords 2000; Hargreaves and Ferguson 2000; Elam and Bertilsson 2003).

- *The Education Model,* which involves the gaining of reliable knowledge by an elite of scientists and its subsequent dissemination to those with knowledge "deficits" contributing to their enlightenment and competence as citizens;

- *The Public Relations Model,* which seeks to improve the public image of science in order to secure its license to practice and increase social and political support for science, science spending and science legislation. A higher profile of some sciences (though probably not archaeology) promises to create additional social wealth as a result too;

- *The Democratic Model,* which emphasises scientific responsibility and sustainable development and is based on participatory processes in which non-scientists predominate.

According to each model scientists have reason to be concerned about the relations between science and society. Followers of the first model tend to lament about a widespread scientific illiteracy that prevents people from making informed choices in our knowledge-based society and they like pointing out scientific inaccuracies in media representations. Those subscribing to the second model often complain about distorted media coverage of science damaging its reputation and thus its interests in society. Finally, supporters of the third model are worried about state-supported scientists being 'illiterate' about the real world themselves and acting against citizens' interests or desires by pursuing unwanted or even dangerous research beyond the realm of proper, democratic accountability.

Although they emerged at different times, all three models are co-existing and competing, although they can be combined both in a single person's outlook and in any chosen strategy. Each model has nevertheless led to a distinctive way of science engaging with the public. The elitist Education Model implies that science holds "a monopoly on truth in society" and is seeking to transmit that truth and its context as accurately as possible to large, passive audiences in accessible formats – often being frustrated by the independence of the media (Weingart 1998: 869-70; cf. House of Lords 2000: chapter 7). The Public Relations Model, in turn, is based on the understanding that in order to maintain or increase public support for science it is essential to win the hearts and minds of large sections of the population through intensive lobbying (Kirby 2003: 242-6). Typical are reminders that

"in modern democratic conditions, science like any other player in the public arena ignores public attitudes and values at its peril. Our recommendation for increased and integrated dialogue with the public is intended to *secure* science's 'licence to practise', not to *restrict* it." (House of Lords 2000: 5.50)

The Democratic Model, finally, recognizes that, in a democratic system, science must answer to peoples' needs, address their desires and concerns and be subjected to political control by non-scientists – even though citizens may occasionally decide against what the experts would deem to be in their best interest.

It is revealing to compare which images of human beings are implied in each model. Whereas the last model implies a view of "the public" as citizens who are essentially able to form their own mature opinions about difficult questions, the former two models depict people as ignorant or incompetent: malleable by media representations and, if left for themselves, unable to gain viable knowledge or make competent judgments about either reality or science. The choice between the three models is thus also a choice between some major political philosophies.

The attitudes and approaches underlying these three basic models can also be discerned in archaeologists' existing evaluations of the way they are portrayed in popular culture (see also Merriman 2004).

The Education Model

Following the intellectual tradition of the Enlightenment, many archaeologists today would agree that the discipline of archaeology primarily aims at re-constructing the past as well as possible, using rational and scientific approaches, methodologies and techniques. The archaeological knowledge gained is then meant to be conveyed, through public education and outreach, to the rest of society.

It causes professional archaeologists much headache when alternative, non-scientific accounts, approaches or representations of their field and profession appear to master more public interest and command larger audiences than their own. The underlying concern is that people get a wrong image, for example because of the "seductions of pseudo-archaeology" and the "lure of bogus archaeology", as *Archaeology Magazine* recently titled

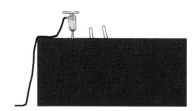

a cover story (May/June 2003). The professionals' answer is usually that 'we need to get better at communicating archaeology' (e.g. Cleere 1988) but, at least in parts, they really mean that 'all others need to get better at listening to us'. What is needed is often defined as "missionary work" by archaeologists (Jordan 1981: 212).

The aim is that as many people as possible will come to see both the past and the occupation of the archaeologist in the same terms as the professional archaeologists themselves. This is what was meant when Warwick Bray (1981) spoke of the need to bridge "the comprehension gap" between what archaeologists think they are doing and what most people believe they actually do. Stereotypes that abound in popular culture (see chapter 5) are dismissed in as much as they are "false" or "not realistic". Archaeologists like Stig Welinder (1987, 1997) believe that a mass audience needs to be protected from such clichés and advocate instead that they be made more familiar with the scientific theory of archaeology and the arguments in current academic debates among professionals.

> "The commodification and glamorization of the excavation of human remains has gone on long enough, and it's difficult enough to battle public stereotypes fueled by Indiana Jones and Lara Croft without having also to witness the promulgation of the filmic fetish with dead bodies in the documentary sector. ... Sensationalism always finds a foothold with the inexperienced and naïve. ... [T]he history of public portrayals of archaeology and the archaeologist have done no service to the past, nor to the present. ... Perhaps the public would be served by a program which does not inflate the artifact or the archaeologist-cum-tomb-raider, but would espouse the responsibilities and sensibilities necessary to writing a meaningful history for present people out of the silent, enduring fragments of the past."
>
> Adam Fish, email to WAC list 2003

There is a particularly strong resentment of "sloppy journalism". Archaeologists sometimes feel helpless against misrepresentations in the mass media despite their best attempts at explaining to journalists why their sites are important and what their work is about. Much gets lost and some gets altered in the translation from science to the media and popular culture. All archaeologists seem to be able to do is invite the journalists back and "hope for the best", as one frustrated colleague wrote in a message to an archaeological discussion group in 2003.

> "Personally I think pseudoarchaeology has done a great deal of damage to the public image of archaeologists. For example, when I am flying anywhere, I am careful not to mention my area of specialization to whoever I am sitting beside because 99% of the time I will be stuck for several hours dealing with someone who thinks the Egyptians had extraterrestrial help building the pyramids! There are plenty of true, fantastic discoveries out there, but the popular press are more interested in sensationalism than fact. I am working on Iron Age gold mines in Yemen that have generated considerable media interest. Not because the technology is interesting, or because there was a fairly advanced (and relatively unknown) civilization there, but only because of the King Solomon's/Queen of Sheba angle. I have thus far refused to co-operate with any of the documentary producers pushing this idea. I see no reason to add more garbage to the public perception of 'Indiana Jones' style archaeology!"
>
> Leanne Mallory, email correspondence 2003

Over the past few decades a constant stream of papers on the challenges of public education and outreach has been published suggesting ever new ways to remedy the present situation and get the archaeological messages better across to more people, more effectively. According to some of these suggestions, archaeologists should

- discuss problematic popular culture portrayals of archaeology in student classes in order to challenge students to rethink their own preconceptions and ultimately "diffuse the power of our rivals" (Baxter 2002b: 29);

- work with popular stereotypes, seeking to educate people about the realities of genuine archaeology by using the evocative imagery of archaeology that abounds in popular culture, not the least in Hollywood films (Sandberg 2006; cf. Russell 2002b: 53);

- catch the interest of wide audiences through, for example, popular re-enactment and then educate them properly later (Näsman 1989);

- present their own views in easily accessible places and formats such as the extensive web pages of *In the Hall of Ma'at*, as proposed by those running it;[46]

- convince their audiences by using humour and make them laugh more (Bray 1981: 228; de Boer 2004: 122-3);

- take a stronger role in educating film producers about their field while at the same time learning to communicate through film and television media themselves (Pohl 1996; Frank 2003);

- influence the content of interactive entertainment products with archaeological themes, i.e. computer games, so that their (sometimes hidden) messages are more in line with the preferences of professional archaeologists (Watrall 2002);

- focus their interpretations less on spectacular ruins and unusual artefacts and more on landscapes and unexcavated sites, in order to avoid the "Indiana Jones syndrome" (Hoffman 1997: 82);

- seek to change popular perceptions and value systems regarding archaeological sites through coded images, among other means, without letting people realise that they are being manipulated by what is essentially archaeological "propaganda" (Addyman 1990; Pühringer 2000: 88-9).

Regarding the final suggestion, which may well be promising good results, it has to be said however that the Education model is not really compatible with any kind of manipulation or propaganda, unlike the following model I will discuss. According to its own principles of enlightenment, the rational way of arriving at a certain insight or position is always more important than any particular content of that insight or position (cf. Holtorf 2004: 47-48).

There is an important social dimension that needs to be considered in this context too. When the archaeologist Peter Fowler (1977: 188) discerned that the "pseudo-study" of

---

[46] http://www.hallofmaat.com

archaeological sites and topics presents "an increasingly attractive model of the past to the disillusioned, anarchic element in the outlook of modern society", it is compelling to rejoin that maybe scientific archaeology, in turn, presents an attractive model of the past to the still believing, obedient element in the outlook of modern society. There can be little doubt that the attractiveness of different archaeological approaches to the past to any individual is to a large extent dependent on his or her education, social background and overall value-system.

In an often cited study, the archaeologist Nick Merriman (1991) argued – in line with many other studies – that visits to museums and heritage sites are associated with high culture and expressive of "a cultivated lifestyle". He showed (1991: 30) that people who are highly educated and enjoy high social status are more than twice as likely to visit museums three or more times a year than people with minimum education and low social status. Conversely, the latter are more than three times as likely never to have visited a museum than the former.

Many museums are historical museums. Interest in the past, expressed by visiting a historical museum, may thus have less to do with any *genuine* curiosity about what really happened in the past (which should be fairly equally distributed among people) and more with a perceived need of some people to express social values and attitudes associated with the ideals of the educated middle classes (cf. Schulze 1993: 142-50). That need could also explain the overall very high percentages of people of all backgrounds who agree that "it is worth knowing about the past". The kind of "worth" mentioned there is of course a very different "worth" than if one would ask if it was "worth" spending public funds on investigating the past when it could also be spent on improving health care (Merriman 1991: 23, 100).

Some of the key distinctions that operate in the Education Model

can be summarised in the form of a table. It illustrates how "proper archaeology", which you find in museums, is actually closely linked to a number of socially specific values.

Proper archaeology	Populist archaeology
scientific, truth-orientated	commercial, market-orientated
serious, intellectual, sense	trivial, vulgar, nonsense
the uncomfortable, demanding way	the easy, uncritical way; needs illustration
real satisfaction but can be uninspiring	seemingly satisfying but actually trash
lectures, museum visits	mass media and popular culture
for its own sake	a means for something else
good conscience, moral high ground	bad conscience, morally inferior
pro-active searching for answers	passive reception of information
real insights in ancient cultures	superficial excitement about discoveries
people interested for the right reasons	people interested for the wrong reasons
historical knowledge and consciousness	ignorance about the past
enlightenment, reality	myth, fantasy, entertainment
High Culture, lasting	cultureless, common, transient
true learning and responsible education	harbours risks for the development of youngsters; at best harmless
public outreach by scientists	prostitution; sensationalistic journalism
ordinary people should not be underestimated	the ignorant, uninterested, unappreciative masses; the Mammon

"Proper archaeology" and "populist archaeology" distinguished according to the Education Model. Such phrases are used in Pallottino 1968, Fowler 1977, Borbein 1981, Maier 1981, Cleere 1988, Näsman 1989; Jones and Longstreth 2002 (cf. Maase 2003).

Understanding the way these distinctions work in relation to each other means questioning the general validity of the Education Model. It is obvious that those not yet sufficiently "enlightened" would not recognise themselves on the right column. They are more likely to claim entirely different values and preferences for themselves which are beyond the scope of this book. They would probably also be happy to identify themselves with at least some of the dominant meanings of archaeology in popular culture, as discussed in chapter 5, in a way supporters of the Education Model would not. In sum, as the seemingly self-evident values of "proper archaeology" according to the Education Model are contextualised, their limited applicability to only one section of society becomes obvious.

The Public Relations Model provides an alternative basis for archaeologists engaging with popular culture, avoiding any reference to problematic social distinctions.

The Public Relations Model

Unlike in the case of some other sciences like the biosciences, society and future economic wealth are not likely to depend a great deal on archaeological knowledge about the past. Archaeology and the jobs of very many professional archaeologists, in turn, depend very much on a number of variables in society: the degree to which political authorities support archaeological museums and other archaeological institutions, the political consensus among tax payers, their representatives and certain other benefactors that it is a good thing to spend a fraction of their money on designated archaeological research projects, the social acceptance of existing laws about the protection of cultural heritage, the willingness of developers or others who have to pay for rescue excavations prior to development and trust the rationales for that, the preference of all sorts of people not to vandalise archaeological sites and artefacts but to visit archaeological museums or to study archaeology at institutions of higher education and many more.

What the Swedish archaeologist Göran Burenhult (1975: 239) wrote three decades ago is today as valid as it was then: "In final analysis, archaeology is dependent on the general public attitude towards it". This is echoed in a statement by the American anthropologist John Cole (1980: 23):

"On the selfish, professionalistic level, archaeologists have a stake in building and preserving a public constituency interested in their research if they are to keep their jobs, grants, book sales, and even their data base."

In recent years, this kind of reasoning has been accepted by more and more individual archaeologists (see e.g. Addyman 1987; Cleere 1988; Little 1991: 26-7; Rieche 1996; Smardz 1997; Paynton 2002; Darvill 2004; de Boer 2004: 120-1; Felder et al 2003: 162-4; Sandberg 2006) as well as by institutions like the Council for British Archaeology or the Archaeological Institute of America.[47] By the same token, archaeologists have increasingly understood how much their discipline already owes to a number of key public relation successes in the past. Heinrich Schliemann's self-portrayals, "TV Personalities of the year" like the archaeologists Mortimer Wheeler (in 1954) and Glyn Daniel (in 1955), movie stars like Harrison Ford in the *Indiana Jones* blockbusters, popular TV series like *Time Team* and continuous bestsellers like Ceram's history of archaeology (1980 [1949]) – all helped to create an immense amount of interest and good will in archaeology without which the discipline and its standing would quite simply be unimaginable today. As the literary scholar David Oels (2005: 347) observed, in Germany archaeological non-fiction as represented by Ceram's work has particularly impressed an entire generation (those born before 1960). They frequently recall the ecstatic reading experience they had and still conceptualise archaeology largely as conveyed in those books. In addition, the American Classicist Jon Solomon (1998: 93) certainly has a point when he claims that Hollywood has helped giving archaeology "a higher profile than almost any other academic discipline".

There is a fairly widely held realisation among archaeologists that media exposure is extremely significant for the well-being of their discipline. They are doing their best to get them on their side. The journalist Neal Ascherson (2004) even argued that archaeologists are better at manipulating the media than vice versa. That view puts into perspective the earlier mentioned common complaint by archaeologists that they are at the peril of unpredictable and (as far as they are concerned) misleading reports by "sloppy" journalists.

---

47   http://www.britarch.ac.uk; http://www.archaeological.org

"There is almost nothing that could be described clearly and presented to the public as a socially significant general purpose of archaeological research. That is why I guess that a realistic representation of the variety of archaeological practice could make a disappointing contribution to the public opinion about archaeology. At least the true story about the aims and results of the project I run bores non-specialist visitors to the site after 10 minutes. Fortunately, they do not take decisions on the project funding!"

An archaeologist who prefers not to be named,
email correspondence 2003

Many archaeologists are understandably keen to popularise in particular their own concerns and interests. But since there is no direct link between the amount of knowledge people have of a given subject and the degree to which they are favourably inclined towards that subject, this can occasionally mean that the image conveyed is not entirely realistic. They seem to agree with the German journalist and scientist Karlheinz Steinmüller who stated succinctly in a recent conversation (Beth and Steinmüller 2004: 236) that even "crackpot visions can have a positive effect". And John Cole (1980: 27), for example, argued that even in relation to the most extreme cases of "cult archaeology", i.e. what others would call pseudo-archaeology,

"archaeologists can ill afford to ignore movements so popular with their popular constituency, and they need to react positively on several levels if they are to maintain or broaden their support rather than cede it to cult movements by default."

In other words, even a false image may need to be cultivated if that is what secures public support and interest in an entire discipline, ultimately perhaps even assuring its survival. This kind of reasoning is a far cry from genuine attempts to make all sections of society understand and appreciate the past and the realities of archaeology. It resembles instead the tactics of modern branding and advertising where the actual truth about a product may not be what sells it (Klein 2001: 345-7). It becomes evident that in the Public Relations Model people are sought to be manipulated in order to make their opinions more compatible with the interests of professional archaeology. Peter Addyman (1990: 262; 1987: 12), creator of the successful *Jorvik Viking Centre* (see chapter 2), was not afraid to describe its

116

function as an "effective propaganda machine" that "brainwashed 5% of the population into our view of the Viking age and of archaeology".

It is sometimes assumed in such contexts that once "hooked", people will be motivated to find out what archaeology is *really* like: "enthusiasts can learn the full story later. If we make archaeology too serious from the beginning, we've blown it," wrote John Gowlett (1990: 157). But is the engineering of interest and support on some false pretences really a legitimate strategy of lobbying? Or should archaeologists not simply face the music of public opinion, however worthwhile its professional representatives think archaeological work might be for society if its members only knew 'better'?

The impact of the media on science

The large impact of the media on contemporary society has meant that their depiction of science acquires significance even for communication between scientists themselves (Kirby 2003; Beth and Steinmüller 2004). This significance is notable on two levels. On the one hand, in order to win acclaim by their peers and funding successful scientists increasingly have to become minor media stars as well. As Peter Weingart (1998: 870) phrased it, "prominence in the media competes with reputation in science". Weingart (1998: 875-6) discusses the case of a German academic whose scientific reputation benefited enormously from the interest the German media took in his work: 85% of all scientific citations of a book which he first published in 1987 occurred after the peak of his media presence in 1992.

On the other hand, proponents of competing theories use the suggestive power of media representations as a strategic device to help decide scientific controversies in their favour (Gregory and Miller 1998: 85). For instance, this was the case in *Jurassic Park* and its sequels where science consultant Jack Horner advanced one-sidedly his own disputed theories of bird evolution (Kirby 2003: 252-4). Similarly, among Egyptologists there is an ongoing debate on whether it is possible today to pronounce ancient Egyptian as it was spoken. Since the hieroglyphic script does not use vowels, some scholars argue that any reconstruction is purely speculative. When Stuart T. Smith, an Egyptologist at the University of California in Santa Barbara, was asked to translate dialogues into ancient Egyptian for the recent films *Stargate*, *The Mummy* and *The Mummy Returns*, he advanced a particular, existing model of Egyptian pronunciations, "in the hope that my colleagues might become more familiar with the notion" of spoken ancient Egyptian and thus also become more favourable to that particular line of research (Stuart T Smith, email correspondence 2004).

Arguably, images in popular culture also have a bearing on academic practices and internal politics within disciplines such as archaeology. Meredith Fraser (email correspondence 2003), a doctoral student at the American University in Washington, D.C., found that

"images of archaeologists presented in popular culture tend to downplay the importance of collaborative work in archaeological projects by emphasizing and privileging the role of the individual. This serves to perpetuate epistemological practices that support the hierarchical control of knowledge production (i.e. single directors controlling data from a site)."

Another example is provided by maritime archaeology, often portrayed as "action-man archaeology" or "real Indiana Jones archaeology". Jesse Ransley (2005) argued that the "androcentric" and "masculist" character of that discipline determines not only who is studying the field but pervades its aims and methods too. As a consequence, "we ignore the possibilities of other ways to be male, female, or to be maritime" which limits the potential of the entire field.

Similar issues crop up again in relation to the recruitment of archaeology students and thus ultimately of professional archaeologists. Without any doubt, popular films like *Stargate* (plus the TV series *Stargate SG-1*) and the *Indiana Jones* movies as well as TV documentary series such as *Time Team* have contributed to a steep increase in student numbers in archaeology. Yes, these portrayals of archaeologists did get people interested and it is hardly surprising that some of the hype of TV archaeology resembles university departments' prospectuses (as discussed in chapter 3). But one also needs to ask whether archaeologists should be complicit in misleading students about the content and character of their degree course. Another worry ought to be precisely which kind of additional students are attracted to archaeology in this way. Meredith Fraser (email correspondence 2003) is rightly concerned that

"the portrayal of archaeologists in mainstream popular culture as primarily white, male, heterosexual, 'able-bodied' individuals serves to alienate experiences, identities and individuals that do not conform to this model of the 'ideal archaeologist.' Ultimately, such portrayals have a detrimental effect on both the real and perceived accessibility of archaeology to individuals and communities that are not represented by this 'ideal.'"

This argument is also born out by Jane Baxter's (2002a: 16) experiences with American undergraduate students who, from watching archaeological movies and documentaries, got the impression that archaeology was not for them:

"they consistently stated that these images left them feeling alienated from archaeology as a discipline, that archaeology was an inaccessible discipline to the lay public, and that they themselves probably could never be archaeologists."

In these cases, it is clear that archaeology is not automatically best served by indoctrinated representations that command the largest popular appeal. What is more, effective propaganda machines like films or popular visitor attractions also carry the risk of potential abuse. Peter Addyman (1990: 263) himself had "little doubt that the Jorvik methods of communication can implant whatever messages are formulated" and therefore bring a particular responsibility for the person deciding about these messages. Addyman himself has done the utmost to maintain academic standards in *Jorvik*'s own brainwashing efforts (see chapter 2). Yet, in a way, his integrity was sheer luck for the rest of us, because there is no established way for society to control which precise messages are implanted in visitors through private visitor attractions (provided they are not in direct conflict with the law).

Whereas the Education Model was socially problematic, the Public Relations Model is politically and, by implication, ethically difficult. Arguably, both these models are too exclusive in the sense that they do not necessarily benefit a large enough number of the population. A final alternative is therefore the Democratic Model. That model does not seek to improve existing knowledge, change attitudes of audiences or imply what it takes to be a real archaeologist: instead it expects the professionals to change according to what people actually want from archaeology.

The Democratic Model

According to the Democratic Model, everybody should be invited and indeed encouraged and enabled to develop their own enthusiasm and "grassroots" interest in archaeology. The only limits that apply are those relevant to all social practices in a democracy and they are largely to do with the need to respect the needs and rights of others. Put simply, archaeologists ought to accept how mature adults prefer to depict both the past and archaeology. The professionals do not serve as a special state police force dedicated to eradicate interpretations of both the past and archaeological practice that would be considered "false" or "inappropriate" by a jury of their peers. In addition to the occupations professional archaeologists already carry out, and are being remunerated

for, no intellectual crusades and missions are required in order to make valued contributions to society.

The philosopher Paul Feyerabend (1924-1994) famously argued that in a democratic society, all world views and thinking traditions should enjoy equal status and state support (see Holtorf 2000). According to the "democratic relativism" which Feyerabend proposed, the sciences and academic disciplines offer only *one* possible way of understanding the world (the past) and they ought not be privileged over any alternative ways of interpreting the world (the past). People do not have "deficits" of hegemonic scientific knowledge but specific local and contextual knowledge that is appropriate to their own lives. Consequently, Feyerabend argued for a need to separate the sciences from the state – parallel to the separation of the Church from the state. He suggested, for example, to teach in schools alternative worldviews to the same extent as the sciences. Moreover, he argued for juries of lay people to control the sciences.

Feyerabend's critics pointed to the enormous scientific progress and the numerous practical applications and other benefits we all enjoy as a result of it, but he dismissed them by questioning this very progress and the superiority of the "benefits" it provided to date. In the case of archaeology, critics of a "democratic relativism" have an even more difficult task since virtually no practical – or indeed other – benefits of *particular* archaeological research are easily discernible, whereas the existing more *general* benefits can arguably also be provided by non-scientific or indeed non-academic approaches. Such more general benefits include the joy of witnessing historical stories, the formation of historically founded collective identities, the knowledge about our origins and possible futures and the creation of heritage sites as visitor destinations. Put simply, in this perspective, "the purpose of engaging the public with archaeology is to encourage self-realisation, to enrich people's lives and stimulate reflection and creativity" (Merriman 2004: 7).

120

The degree of openness towards peoples' own understandings and concerns, which was characteristic for Feyerabend's work, is mirrored in some recent work about the relations between science and society. For example, a recent report from the House of Lords (2000) emphasised repeatedly an increased need for dialogue between the sciences and society in order to rebuild the ostensibly damaged public trust in science and scientific experts. That report (chapter 5) speaks of "democratic science", advocates a sea change in increased openness and public dialogue and proposes the participation of lay people in scientific advisory groups, thus implementing precisely some of Feyerabend's ideas. Even the very expression "public understanding of science" is put into question and "science and society" suggested as an alternative: "because it implies dialogue, in a way that 'public understanding of science' does not" (paragraph 3.19). Elsewhere, the phrase "public engagement with science" has been suggested, including even "street marches, boycotts and sit-ins" as legitimate means of action (Elam and Bertilsson 2003).

> "[A]rchaeological research is directed more and more inwards into the society of professional archaeologists itself, while at the same time serving easily digested pictures of the past to the public. Other contesting views of the past thus remain unofficial and outside of the official, authoritative picture produced by professional archaeologists. For many reasons, as we have seen, this can no longer be justified. ... All voices demand to be heard, and if archaeology continues to deny such contesting pasts through means of ignorance, it is archaeology that will ultimately become marginalised and portrayed as an anecdote by the world.... It seems that archaeology must meet the world, and take the consequences of such a meeting by changing from within. There is a long way to go, recognising the problem is only a start."
>
> Anna Källén (2004: 114)

A similar change of heart can be found in some recent archaeological statements and debates. For example, "The Principles for Good Archaeological Practice" of *The Swedish Archaeological Society* mention the need for archaeologists not only "to inform the public" but also to "engage the local and/or indigenous people in the planning and execution" of archaeological projects (Broadbent 2004). This intention was mirrored in a recent policy review of the Swedish heritage sector, known as *Agenda Kulturarv* (2004). The resulting policy statement expressed the need to explain and refine, in co-operation with all stakeholders in the sector, the how, what and why of heritage management: "We must make the public's involvement and participation

121

our top priorities" (2004: 16). Similar thinking, highlighting the importance of dialogue between professionals and "the public", has long informed cultural politics and its express aims. Unfortunately, the realities of archaeology do not always appear to have corresponded with these high ambitions. Arguably, the professionals have tended to prefer their own monologue, conducted in isolation, to a constructive and open-minded dialogue with a broad constituency of interested citizens (Gustafsson and Karlsson 2004).

A truly democratic approach can go even further than dialogue though. The Swedish archaeologists Håkan Karlsson and Björn Nilsson (2000: 23, all my translations) argued that "everybody has a right to have their own history", that state heritage management must serve everybody equally and that academic archaeology is nothing but a very specific phenomenon, relative to a particular context and not inherently valuable to everybody. People are interested in archaeology for other reasons than what some professionals tend to believe. Karlsson and Nilsson went on to conclude (2000: 39) that "arguably the public is interested [in archaeology] not as a result of [professional] archaeology's successful public outreach but rather despite of it." Their argument can be read to imply that it is the public that should have the final say about what professional archaeologists do and not do.

In this view, fundamental changes in the public relations of professional archaeology are

- "Thanks to the americans and their friends, we can now all own a little piece of our history!"

necessary. In a truly democratic society, professional archaeologists need to address the reasons why people are actually interested in both the past and in archaeology. They need to work together with non-specialists whenever possible. And they need to get worried indeed when alternative approaches to the past are becoming more successful in satisfying what people want to get out of archaeology (Fowler 1977: 189). For example, concerning Egyptology in the public domain it is now the alternative camp of Bauval, Hancock & Co. that appears to have a clear edge over the academic discipline (Picknett and Prince 2003: 190-2). It is thus the professionals who need to be willing to learn. Arguably, this should happen sooner rather than later (Karlsson and Nilsson 2000: 21):

> "At the present time it appears that [professional] Swedish archaeology is exploiting a great trust among the interested public. The question is though for how long the public is going to accept to be passively fed with our knowledge, and for how long people outside the professional sphere are going to tolerate our lack of interest in their interest."

This position may sound very persuasive at first but it is certainly not without its problems. There is a risk that too much is asked if people are to decide for themselves what the past was like and what archaeology is supposed to be doing. Competent decisions in these fields might require a degree of expertise that *de facto* only few non-professionals will ever acquire. But even when the issues at stake may be less complex, it is pertinent to consider that "you can't assume that people know what they want" (Packard 1960: 18). Any decisions taken democratically risk to reflect little else but superficial preferences based practically entirely on current TV programmes, Hollywood blockbusters or misunderstood popular science literature, while at the same time valuable historical sites may be irretrievably destroyed and opportunities for others to learn more about both academic archaeology and its results may be dramatically reduced.

On the other hand, even if that should happen, precisely what would we lose? Just as it is wrong to assume that everything that results in raising the gross national product is good for a particular country and its people (cf. Packard 1960: chapter 23), it is also wrong to assume that everything that results in more widespread knowledge about academic science or in preserving more ancient sites is necessarily good for them either. There are alternative benefits to be gained from being more democratic. Professional archaeology is neither rocket science nor essential plumbing or emergency surgery. Even if the Democratic Model will result in some setbacks for the field as it exists at the moment, the benefits from truly engaging more people and providing them with memorable archaeological experiences may well make up for them.

"The call for public education has been a recurrent theme in the literature of archaeological heritage management, where both Western and non-Western archaeologists see it as an antidote to 'indifference' and 'apathy' towards the fate of archaeological sites. Posited here, implicitly, is an infantile condition: prior to education a void exists in the public's mind where knowledge of and respect for the material past should be. What I have tried to show in a limited way is that multiple and mature discourses on the material past already exist in the space archaeology depicts as void. What archaeology intends, really, is not education but re-education."

Denis Byrne (1995: 278)

These matters are naturally not easy to resolve and lie at the heart of some far bigger discussions in political science. Ultimately the question is one of how we should best practice democracy and whether that should be some form of direct democracy or not rather a representative democracy. The relevance of that question stretches to all areas of society, not just archaeology. The issue at stake is about finding the right balance between public participation and the possibility of creative self-realisation for as many people as possible on the one hand and on the other hand the need for the state and its agencies to ensure that competent decisions are taken in all areas where, otherwise, public interests might be harmed. What is therefore patronising state propaganda for some, is public education for others. By the same token, what some may perceive as a legitimate expression of peoples' own preferences is a first step towards dangerous anarchy for others.

However that may be, some such political concerns and democratic values certainly sound much less radical when they are applied to indigenous populations. Over more than a decade now, archaeologists have developed considerable – though perhaps still not satisfactory – sensitivity for the rights and interests of indigenous populations

- "Mr Professor sir, I am from the State Planning and Development Department, and I am instructed to show you our new regulations."

in many parts of the world (see e.g. Broadbent 2004). It is beyond question now that such non-professional voices need to be heard by archaeologists and increasingly they are also being listened to.

As far as the meaning of archaeology in Western popular culture is concerned, there is thus an important distinction between people in the West and people elsewhere, whether indigenous or not. Whereas the former are, however indirectly, driving the meanings of archaeology that abound in contemporary popular culture, the latter are unable to advance to the same extent their own desired versions of archaeology.

The Democratic Model has thus two very different consequences under these two very different conditions. Regarding the Western world, a democratic approach broadly defends popular culture against the interests of a narrow concern with the sciences and academic disciplines. Regarding the rest of the world, a democratic approach scrutinizes Western popular culture for messages that harm the legitimate rights and interests of non-Western societies. Since Western popular culture does not at all rely on derogative messages about other people, both strategies are not contradictory but rather complementary.

Common components of popular archaeology are notions of exotic places full of natives some of whom help Western archaeologists recover lost pasts, reveal mysteries, unearth treasures and demonstrate how primitive conditions have once before been overcome. Combined with "the heroizing of an archaeology that can accomplish such wonders through the glories of western science," such notions legitimate a very problematic view of modernisation and a particular view of archaeology contributing to that process (Cohodas 2003). Although, in Western democratic societies, audiences are certainly free to choose by which stereotypical heroes they wish to be entertained and how they prefer to interpret the world, some of these notions are hardly in the interest of the local people implicated. On that account they need to be challenged. As the Canadian anthropologist Marvin Cohodas (2003) argued, even if some established parameters will need to be modified, archaeological hero stories can still be told and they can still be exciting for Western audiences:

> "I realize that in the present situation, neither archaeologists nor the media want to surrender the construction of archaeologists as heroes. So, I propose a compromise. Let archaeologists continue to be heroes. Let them be rewarded for great heroic efforts and

125

applauded by the public as well as granted funds to continue and increase their heroism. But let us measure that heroism by a different standard. Let archaeologists be deemed heroes when they advance the cause of the Indigenous Peoples who are the descendants and inheritors of the past that they excavate and interpret. Let them be heroes when they ask these descendants what kind of archaeology might serve their purposes, when they consult about the questions to be asked and the methods to be used to seek to answer them. Let archaeologists be heroes when they train indigenous archaeologists and treat them as colleagues, encouraging and empowering a strong aboriginal voice in the collaborative formation, nature, and dissemination of interpretation. Let them be heroes when they respect the knowledge of Indigenous Peoples who are not archaeologists."

That, too, is a position that follows from the Democratic Model. And that is another reason why I have particular sympathies with this model, although I would certainly not want to dismiss completely any of the other two models either.

Time Team **and the three models**

The British TV series *Time Team* as well as other well-funded TV documentaries (see chapter 3) are operating on a scale that their impact on archaeology is no longer restricted to how they inform, shape or express public opinion. Instead, the productions themselves generate sufficient new data and analysis to have a notable impact on existing academic archaeology. *Time Team* itself has led to much new research published in an impressive number of archaeological reports and papers.[48] Having said that, it is illuminating, in the way of a summary of this chapter, to compare how each of the three models applies to *Time Team*.

According to the British heritage expert Henry Cleere (2000), Time Team "presents a somewhat distorted and over-simplified picture of what archaeology is really about." He argues that "[t]he time has now surely come to have enough confidence in the appeal of the subject ... to modify the format slightly so as to present a more balanced and honest picture." According to Cleere, "the potential is there for something that will improve the quality without losing the ratings." Significantly, quality is here signified by an accurate picture of what archaeology is about. Moreover, this picture ought to be perfected once that commercial necessity, the ratings, are satisfactory. This is a position typical for proponents of the Education Model.

---

[48] http://www.channel4.com/history/timeteam/reports.html

John Walker, Chief Executive of the York Archaeological Trust, on the other hand is a follower of the Public Relations Model. When I met him in York (see chapter 2), he stated that the most important role of *Time Team* in relation to archaeology was its usefulness in the field of politics. In his experience, the popularity of the TV series helped to convince politicians that archaeology is important and worthwhile to take into account. *Time Team* has changed the image of archaeology from stuffy to cool and broadened the popular appeal of archaeology in the UK considerably. Mike Heyworth of the Council for British Archaeology explained the value of that change by speculating whether a future Chancellor of the Exchequer (i.e. British Finance Minister) may be more sympathetic to the desires of archaeologists because he is now an enthusiastic watcher of *Time Team*.

> "The net result of all the TV archaeology is that my job as a curator is made easier because virtually everyone who comes to us with a planning application now understands at least the basic issues surrounding archaeology (although I do get a bit tired of the agents for developers proving how their developer is sensitive by telling me how much they enjoy watching *Time Team*!)"
>
> Vince Russett, email to the discussion group *britarch* (2003)[49]

George, an archaeology enthusiast, never submitted his 'Big Dig' findings but did have to contact the Water Board.

Finally, in line with the Democratic Model, one can consider the popular *Time Team* format as representing something like an archaeology of the people. This was certainly born out with the *The Big Dig* project in the summer of 2003 (see chapter 3). As the official web diary of the event recalls, loads of people enjoyed joining the experts in their investigations of the British past.[50] *Time Team* archaeologist Mick Aston (under the entry for Sunday, 22 June 2003) is reported to have said about his experience in the village of Great Easton in Leicestershire:

---

49 http://www.jiscmail.ac.uk/cgi-bin/webadmin?A2=ind0311&L=britarch&P=R8950&I=-1
50 http://www.channel4.com/history/microsites/B/bigdig/diary/index.html

"I walked down the High Street with Tim Taylor at lunch time and nearly every garden had people digging a hole and filling out recording sheets. It's brilliant to see so many people getting involved with their archaeology. This really is what it's all about. People learning about and enjoying their past in a constructive way."

Francis Pryor, too, liked this initiative and had this to say about its critics: "I smell elitism and self interest and I don't like it" (*The Guardian*, 21 June 2003). The event would arguably have been even less elitist and more democratic if people had actually been allowed and encouraged to do anything *they wanted* with the finds from their back gardens!

So where do we go from here? Which model do I offer as the way forward regarding archaeology's awkward relationship with its meaning in popular culture? The Education Model, the Public Relations Model and the Democratic Model each provide very different strategies for archaeology's public relations. The point of this book is not to choose

128

between them but to ensure that future debates among professional archaeologists on this issue can make reference to the specific arguments, both in favour and against, that characterise each of these models. Indeed, much might be said for combining elements of all these models into future strategies of archaeology engaging with the public. These discussions will have to go hand in hand with further considerations of the aims of archaeology in society, as these have a large impact on how to engage with the meaning of archaeology in popular culture.

The final chapter of the book will sum up the argument presented in this book and mention a few archaeological projects and initiatives that I find particularly interesting and indeed promising for the future development of public archaeology.

Chapter 7

Public archaeology reconsidered

So what are archaeologists to make of their portrayal in contemporary popular culture? In the previous six chapters I surveyed a number of key realms, some empirical and some theoretical.

From the perspective of the tourist (chapter 2), the TV watcher and the newspaper reader (chapter 3), it is hard to avoid the conclusion that archaeology is everywhere and that it is one of the most appealing themes of our age. With reference to the trends in society that I discussed in chapter 1, one might say that archaeology provides particularly engaging experiences for the Experience Society and extremely evocative stories for the Dream Society. In other words, archaeology is a very trendy subject in the Western world and far more than the speciality interest of a few. But in stating that, what kind of archaeology am I actually referring to?

The currency of archaeology is rooted in a few key stereotypes and clichés of the discipline which, individually or combined, evoke what I have been calling "archaeo-appeal" (Holtorf 2005: chapter 9). In this book I distinguished (in chapter 5) four particularly important themes that characterize the meaning of archaeology in popular culture. According to the A theme, archaeologists are heroes who go through exciting adventures in exotic locations. In the D theme, they are detectives and scholars who

- "Oh this, we find this sort of stuff all the time"

successfully solve their cases by knowing how to find and read clues in the right way. Archaeologists can also miraculously bring the past back to life and may be able to reveal some great truths for the benefit of humankind reassuring us about our prospects – which I called the R theme. Closer to home, according to the C theme, archaeologists rescue precious sites and artefacts from obliteration so that academics and others can appreciate them even in the future. Significantly, these grand four themes do not only involve the intellect but also our bodies and emotions. Archaeology is about the hardship of fieldwork, the longing for treasures and the joys of discovery. It is about the satisfaction of putting one more puzzle piece into place and suddenly seeing a larger picture. It is about the intricate practicalities of running a rescue excavation and saving archaeological heritage from imminent destruction while being under pressure from all directions. For many archaeologists, both in popular culture and in reality, all this together constitutes a way of life. Sometimes, others consider it an enviable way of life.

These stereotypical clichés that have come to dominate the public perception of the discipline share the feature that they all present archaeology in metaphorical rather than literal terms. By that I mean that in each theme archaeology comes to stand for something other than what it purports to be in concrete terms. It is not normally the specific site being investigated, the specific clue being discovered, the specific insight being gained, or the specific artefact being rescued that matter a great deal in their own right. Instead, the specifics only matter in so far as they become elements in larger stories simultaneously being told about great adventure, detective work, quests for answering Big Questions, or careful and responsible resource management.

What all four themes share too, is their emphasis on archaeology as a process, that is on "doing" archaeology rather than on the actual results being produced. There is very little appreciation in popular culture of the fact that archaeologists can tell us in some detail what specifically went on in the past and far more emphasis is given to how they arrive at any specific insight, notably through digging up artefacts and piecing together various kinds of available evidence (see chapters 3 and 5). Even indoor museums, like the Archaeological State Museum in Konstanz (Germany), have understood that a simulated excavation site evokes an appealing archaeological atmosphere that provides a particularly favourable scene for presenting archaeological exhibits and displays. That fascination with the practice of archaeology was also born out in the existing surveys of peoples' attitudes towards archaeology, as shown in chapter 4. The most common association people have with "archaeology" is invariably the notion of digging up things

and because of this particular archaeo-appeal many would enjoy getting into archaeology themselves. Other scientific fields, like anthropology (MacClancy 2005), physics, chemistry and psychoanalysis, share with archaeology a popular emphasis on the way they are being *done*. On the other hand, in the popular perceptions of engineering, meteorology or ecology it matters a lot more precisely what knowledge the experts arrive at.

Are there, then, any significant differences between the three countries of Sweden, the U. K. and Germany which I focused on in my research? Except from chapter 3 when I discerned slightly diverging profiles of archaeology in these nations' national TV schedules, especially regarding the very significant role of *Time Team* in the U.K., I did not say a great deal about such differences in other chapters. The reason for that is that I do not think that any existing differences in the relative importance of certain stereotypes are very large. In any case, they did not emerge prominently from the qualitative methodology I mostly worked with. My examples were chosen from all three countries, as they seemed to illustrate each point best. Among them, you will however find a stronger representation of films that were originally published in English. That is hardly surprising since so much of contemporary Western popular culture – for better or worse – has its roots in Hollywood. The extent to which Hollywood at the same time has become appropriated around the world became clear to me when I heard of the Hong Kong produced movie *Undiscovered Tomb* (2002) which has been described as "Asia's Tomb Raider".[51]

As I argued in chapter 6, it is a disputed issue how professional archaeologists should react toward the existing clichés of archaeology. Drawing on some recent discussion within science studies and science policy debates, I distinguished three approaches that summarise the principal positions available to professional archaeologists – assuming that one does not wish to ignore the phenomenon entirely. According to the Education Model, the public simply needs to be better informed and enlightened about what archaeology *really* is. The Public Relations Model, on the other hand, insists that public opinion matters in relation to the public image of archaeology which in turn affects the degree of political support archaeologists can expect to receive for their work. Finally, the Democratic Model emphasises that archaeology will serve the people best if it actually allows them to participate in setting the agenda for professional archaeology, according to their own preferences and desires. Arguably, these popular preferences and desires are indicated (though perhaps not exhausted) by the realities of how archaeology is presented in existing popular culture.

---

[51] http://hkfilm.net/movrevs2/untomb.htm

The aim of my discussion was not to suggest any simple strategy by which professional archaeologists could determine the single best response to, for instance, a new Indiana Jones movie. Instead, I hope that future discussions among professionals will be helped by the possibility to refer to a set of well-defined models defining the principal positions available. All sorts of hybrid positions are likely to emerge in relation to specific cases. There is, however, one aspect that I wish all archaeologists would take to heart more than they have until now. That is the realisation that in the public domain archaeology is a very successful brand!

Archaeology as a brand

Few disciplines are lucky enough to be similarly widely and similarly positively represented in popular culture as archaeology is. The brand of archaeology is associated with so many positive appeals, stories and dreams that other brands, despite their sometimes vast advertising budgets, can only envy (see also chapter 1). It is simply not true, as Miles Russell (2002b: 46) claimed that "the pop culture archaeologist is systematically portrayed as 'the bad guy'." In fact, one could hardly imagine archaeology's image to be more favourable than it already is.

Although each of the four themes also has some problematic sides, as I pointed out in my discussion (chapter 5), the archaeologists' image overall in Western popular culture is extremely flattering. When archaeologists are very occasionally portrayed as unscrupulous and presumptuous, interfering with people's or ancestors' legitimate demands, these are minor aspects of an otherwise extremely positive image of archaeology revolving around adventure, detective work, profound revelations and care. In contrast, the popular characterisations of other popular disciplines – like the sciences, medicine or law – have dangerous, dull, or generally dubious sides that are far more accentuated and firmly integrated into their overall image, thus significantly diminishing the very strong appeal of, for example, physicists, doctors or lawyers (Haynes 1994).

If brands are like persons, archaeology comes across as a person you would intuitively like to have as a good friend and maybe spend your holidays with. What is more, archaeology can actually deliver much of what its brand promises. In other words, archaeology can make people enjoy themselves and satisfy some of their innermost wishes and desires. Each archaeological company or institution is thus not in the business of understanding the

> "People everywhere are fascinated by archaeology. Archaeologists know it. We are all familiar with exclamations like 'Oh, how interesting,' or 'How lucky you are,' when a new acquaintance learns of our profession. We are accustomed to fielding questions like 'What's the oldest (weirdest, most interesting, or most valuable) thing you've found?' Each of us has developed a set of polite responses to these questions – responses we hope are not patronizing, misleading, or didactic."
>
> Kevin Jones and Julie Longstreth (2002: 187)

past but of enhancing people's lives through adventures, mysteries, revelations and offering possibilities to care. Brands do not rely on culture and lifestyle but they are culture and lifestyle (Klein 2001).

Archaeology's positive appeal provides an enormous opportunity for the entire discipline because it helps build a huge support network on which it can rely. There is one crucial condition for all this though. Archaeologists will only be able to use the enormous appeal of their own brand if they themselves stand behind it and embrace its various connotations in their work. It simply astonishes me that a fairly large proportion of archaeologists still seem to find nothing more urgent than to distance themselves from popular heroes like Indiana Jones or Lara Croft. It is deeply ironic that nothing seems to be harder for archaeologists to get to grips with in their relations with non-archaeologists than their seemingly limitless and virtually untainted overall popularity that is unrivalled among academic disciplines.

I have given up counting the number of exhibitions, educational events and publications (e.g. Robinson and Aston 2002) that are shouting into the reader's face that "the real archaeologist works practically never like Indiana Jones/Lara Croft." Translated, that means as much as "If you happen to be interested in archaeology because of Indiana Jones/Lara Croft, then this is not for you!" Archaeology is thus suddenly outed as a different kind of 'person' than you thought and hoped it was; a person that lacks some of the traits you found most appealing. It is the equivalent to Greenpeace beginning a public presentation about its work by stating that "the real Greenpeace activist works practically never in a small rubber-dinghy fighting illegal whalers." Although true, this would achieve nothing except alienate an initially favourable audience before it has had an opportunity to hear what it is you *actually* want to convey.

What is smarter is to build on the existing brand appeal of archaeology, including its bodily and emotional dimensions, in order to celebrate, modify or extend its content. Professional archaeologists can use existing trends and established brand qualities in many ways to their own advantage. For example, I was struck by the web page design of the *Register of Professional Archaeologists* in the United States.[52] The first association

---

[52] http://www.rpanet.org

134

that comes to mind are *Stargate* and various dimensions of the R theme. Similarly, *Archaeology Magazine*, published by the Archaeological Institute of America, has long been great at anchoring its stories in the A and D themes.[53] Such deliberate uses of archaeo-appeal are in line with the "Walker Maxim" which states that professional archaeologists should use the public image of archaeology to their own advantage (as discussed in chapter 5). In a move that John Walker would probably also approve of, a British Professor of Archaeology, Clive Gamble (2001: 1), began his basic introduction to the discipline with the somewhat unacademic statement that "Archaeology is about excitement."

By the same token, in an exhibition entitled "Buried Treasure", the *British Museum* deliberately embraced the cliché that archaeology is about treasures and even featured a Lara Croft-like heroine.[54] Likewise referring to the popular tomb raider, *National Geographic News* recently published an article about new technology used by archaeologists, boldly claiming that "Lara Croft will have to shop for some better gadgetry if she wants to keep up with her archaeological peers".[55] In Stockholm, the Museum of National Antiquities created a role-playing game in which a battle about history takes place in an entirely fictitious Swedish Museum of National Antiquities: "There are heroes, villains and innocent bystanders – all knowingly or unknowingly involved in the ongoing conflict between some secretive and terrifying forces".[56] In a similar bow to popular trends and preferences, a new archaeological museum in Germany draws the visitor into an imaginative criminal investigation as its central theme (see chapter 5; Derks 2003). All these examples illustrate how it is possible to draw on qualities already associated with the brand of archaeology in a constructive and compelling way.

Let people dig!

As I discussed earlier (chapter 4), a large number of people are excited about the process of archaeological research and would like to get involved in archaeological projects themselves. Especially the digging aspect is enormously appealing. The Canadian archaeologist Karolyn Smardz (1997: 103) once speculated about the reasons for the popularity of archaeological excavations, which by the way may also account for the popularity of modern treasure-hunting (Merriman 1991: 106):

---

53 http://www.archaeology.org
54 http://www.thebritishmuseum.ac.uk/buriedtreasure
55 http://news.nationalgeographic.com/news/2003/07/0731_030731_tomb.html
56 my translation from http://www.historiska.se/histvarld/sourcesida.htm

"It is the excitement and romance of archaeological discovery that makes people think archaeology is worth doing and learning about. [...] In other words, it is not archaeology's ability to help all of us gain a better understanding of how people lived in the past that makes archaeology marketable, it is also that mysterious, romantic, exotic sense of delving into the unknown – *ergo*, the very process of archaeological research."

The popular desire to dig can easily be satisfied through digitally simulated excavations as offered, for example, by the national Swedish television station SVT[57]. In addition, there are more and more actual archaeological field projects, where anybody is invited to come along and become practically involved. Open Days on on-going excavations, whether as part of nation-wide Archaeology Days or locally organised, are regular features in the calendar of many archaeological projects and they are often highly popular and well attended. Occasionally, even the excavation sites themselves are deliberately chosen with participation of community members, including school children, in mind (e.g. Smardz 1997). Whereas in York, you can spend "A Day on the Dig" (see chapter 2), in Germany and Austria paying tourists can take part in regular excavation projects for longer periods.[58] One of these initiatives advertises in the following way[59]:

"Adventure Archaeology. Join the investigations! Holidays on a research excavation in the ancient homeland of the Celts. [...] During a week-long adventure holiday – excavation and attractive sightseeing programme – you can experience how archaeologists assemble a colourful image of the past from numerous mosaic stones. And you are participating yourself – in a very find-rich area."

Interestingly, many people are willing to pay a small fee, even in exchange for merely being able to observe archaeologists at work, as Peter Addyman (1990: 258) found when well over half a million people (between 1976 and 1981) came to see his excavations at York, although he charged them for the opportunity. Since then, this interest has not waned. It is clear that (a) if an offered experience is perceived as enjoyable and worthwhile, people are willing to pay for it and that (b) once you hope to attract paying visitors you automatically focus more on what kind of engaging experience you might be able to stage (Pine and Gilmore 1999: 61-68). Charging visitors can therefore not only help archaeology financially but also create an improved overall outcome of a given project.

In some circumstances, participation in an archaeological excavation may even acquire therapeutic dimensions. Community archaeology projects can help people deal with traumatic pasts and create a sense of unity (Lucas 2004: 119). This, for example, was one of the functions of the recent excavations in the Swedish village of Södra Råda where, in 2001, a famous 14th century wooden church with exquisite wall paintings had been burned down due to arson.

[57] http://svt.se/svt/jsp/Crosslink.jsp?d=25213&a=297936
[58] http://www.expeditionzone.com
[59] My translation from a site now available at http://web.archive.org/web/20041119122614/http://www.landkreis-landshut.de/landratsamt/presse/arch/seite1.htm

Before the process of re-construction of the church could begin, the Swedish National Heritage Board and two regional museums invited the local community to take part in archaeological investigations on the ground where the church once stood. The Södra Råda project[60] was one way to help people coming to terms with the sense of loss they experienced in the aftermath of the fire, but it was also a pilot project for a new kind of public archaeology. In her report, the project director Catarina Karlsson (2004: 23) stated what can have validity even beyond Södra Råda: since archaeology is important not for its own sake but for peoples' sakes, an archaeological project becomes the more significant the more people enjoy the project and participate in it.

Letting people dig is a great way of bringing archaeology to the people. It allows them to enjoy archaeology in the way they prefer it.

Mrs Cynthia Fullbloom of Haselby's WI is this season's gold winner of the best kept trowelled area. She also won the bronze trophy in the category of mattocking in confined areas.

---

[60] http://www.sodrarada.se

Of course, in many ways the reality of professional archaeology is not entirely different from the stereotypical clichés of archaeology that are so prominent in popular culture. Each theme has at least *some* relation to what the professionals really do, even to how they see themselves, although there are also many aspects of their work that are not reflected in any of these themes. Archaeologists really do find exciting treasures and their fieldwork really is often exciting enough. Precisely that adventure aspect is central even to how many archaeologists define themselves and how they prefer to work and remember their work (Welinder 1987: 36-8; 2000: chapter 4; Holmgren and Kaliff 2003; de Boer 2004; Holtorf 2005: chapter 3). Archaeologists love Indiana Jones.[61] Further, professional archaeologists really can reconstruct parts of the past from seemingly insignificant clues and learn about the lives of people in the past, using modern scientific methodologies. It has been called (Sebastian 2003: 36) an "awful truth about archaeology" that

> "[it] is exciting because it connects with the past in a way that nothing else can, and sometimes that connection can be stunningly immediate and personal."

Archaeologists can even succeed in providing us occasionally with seemingly supernatural experiences when they bring us in direct contact with people that are long dead. And very occasionally, archaeology really can deliver profound insights about issues like the course of history and the future prospects of the human species. Finally, archaeologists certainly are taking care of ancient remains in and on behalf of society, getting into numerous 'fights' with adversaries that do not put the same value on the same remains (Welinder 2000: 87). The A, D, R and C themes are thus not entirely fictitious but contain a true core. Just as their popular culture counterparts, archaeologists enjoy the excitement of doing archaeological fieldwork. They love discovering artefacts, investigating questions about past mysteries through meticulous empirical study and scientific analysis, pondering Big Questions about human history on planet Earth and saving precious information from sites that are doomed to be destroyed. In sum, as Clive Gamble (2001: xiii) informed archaeological novices, archaeology is "one of the most important and fascinating topics you could ever hope to encounter" and "nothing is more interesting, more stimulating or more rewarding than the study of archaeology."

---

61 http://www.archaeologyfieldwork.com/cgi-bin/yabb/YaBB.cgi?board=survey;action=display;num=10799054
53

Outlook: reconfiguring public archaeology

When I began my research on the topic of this book, several well-meaning colleagues understood that I was trying to assess archaeologists' efforts at educating a larger public about archaeology. They recommended me to read specific books written by academic authors and to study how some professionals were contributing to public education in the mass media – as if any of that could reveal very much about my topic, the meaning of archaeology in popular culture. The most important question that archaeologists in public contexts need to ask their audiences is not "How can I best persuade you about the merits of my project or discipline?" but "What does what I am doing mean to you?" (Ascherson 2004: 157). Yet, to date, these meanings have not very often been investigated by archaeologists (significant exceptions include Kirchner 1964; Pallottino 1968; Welinder 1987; Jensen and Wieczorek 2002).

Archaeologists have still not properly come to terms with the popularity of their own subject in the mainstream. In parts, this may be because some academics prefer studying lasting cultural achievements to an encounter with the pleasurable frivolity and superficiality of

popular culture (cf. Maase 2003). But if we want to understand how people now are appreciating archaeology within the worlds in which they live, it is inevitable to study archaeology within that very context. Ascherson's new question ultimately leads to a new paradigm for public archaeology (see also Holtorf 2005). In order to get better at public archaeology, professional archaeologists will need to try and work *with* rather than *against* the pre-understandings and expectations of their non-archaeological audiences. It has become pertinent, or even urgent to try and relate archaeology

to "what's hot and what's cool in the world beyond the professional and academic boundaries of the discipline" (Darvill 2004: 57).

Any possible benefits of a purely academic understanding of archaeology – different from its popular appeal – are not obvious to the rest of the population. As a group of Swedish students (André et al 2001) demonstrated in a thought experiment, it is all too easy to argue that archaeology is a pretty useless and unsuccessful academic discipline that tells us very little of a highly hypothetical nature about issues of little relevance to us today. Arguably, archaeology produces little else than artefacts that end up in dark storage vaults and literature, such as excavation reports, that not very many people will ever read. At the same time, money is lacking for health care, social security, education, how anybody could possibly want to go ahead with archaeology at all. To counter

---

DIGGING FOR 'CULTURAL HERITAGE' MEANINGLESS

One doesn't know whether to cry or throw up. Hundreds of thousands of kronor are being spent on digging at Veddige church, because the 'mafia' *thinks* there may have been some sort of settlement there from the Viking Age, where the Vikings left behind a hearthstone sooty from grilling sausages, a stone used to scrape animal skins, or a blunt stone axe.

How many Swedes with half a brain are actually interested in this rubbish? Soon half of Sweden will have been dug up and the money just keeps pouring into this pointless digging for what is known as 'cultural heritage'. In case the politicians don't know what 'cultural' means, there are reference books available in both Swedish and politician-speak. Who the hell wouldn't want to be cultural? The 'mafia' has got free licence!

A few hundred metres from this nuisance there lies a school, a day care centre, a nursing home and a doctor's surgery, where the low-paid staff work their butts off to make the whole thing work. And here they want to save money by getting rid of the pastries and buns. How much longer will the people put with the excesses of the political mafia?

Those poor politicians don't need to go on strike for higher wages! They give themselves a wage increase of several thousand kronor on a regular basis.

The culture and art mafia must be stopped! Wake up Swedish people! Make some noise!

Tired of people in la-la land

A letter to the editor, from *Hallands Nyheter* 31 May 2003, translated by Ymke Mulder

such alternative energy research, or international solidarity, so that one can only wonder arguments, professional archaeologists must be pro-active and make sure that they fulfil and are seen to fulfil, a social role that is widely appreciated in society. Archaeology must therefore focus on topics and approaches that do not only enjoy wide public appeal but that also draw media attention and volunteers. After all, "overly academic topics will do poorly in a leisure economy" (Moore 2006: 18). This ambition to define archaeology in terms of usefulness and popularity should not be considered as the "prostitution" of an academic discipline. It is rather a reminder of its social duty (see also Rieche 1996).

It does not take more than a good look at the characterisation of archaeology in popular culture as attempted in this book to find out what might be archaeology's most important aim and function in contemporary Western society: archaeology tells us stories that are both exciting and full of important metaphorical meanings. Archaeological stories are about heroes who overcome adversities and solve mysteries. Archaeologists can give meticulous attention to detail. Their research is often about contemplating and perhaps answering, large existential questions or other issues of significance to many people. Archaeologists are taking responsibility of scarce resources for everybody's benefit. Such characters and the stories within which they act matter to people, for they reflect some of their dreams and aspirations but also issues of concern and immediate relevance to their own lives (see also Jensen 2002).

We all live through adventures during which we need to overcome adversity, hoping to emerge as heroes. We all need to attend to detail, occasionally, hoping to solve complex cases. We all wonder about what it all means and where it will all end, hoping to gain some certainties and peace of mind in an uncertain world. We all need to take care of our resources, both personally and on levels of larger communities of, for instance, employees or citizens, hoping that we will manage. In other words, archaeology tells us stories that are directly concerned with ourselves. It is these stories that give archaeology currency in the contemporary world. They show to what extent Western societies are dominated by certain dreams and experiences that transform us as human beings and give our lives meaning (see also chapter 1). In a sense it can be said that the archaeologist is not digging for artefacts but for dreams (Petersson 1994: 71). By the same token, John Fritz (1973: 81) summarized what archaeology contributes to society in the following way:

"archeology is of interest to, rooted in the experience of, and is beneficial to the common [hu]man in several respects. It provides puzzles to be solved, vicarious experience of the

exotic and the adventurous, the hope of 'striking it rich,' and a form of contact with the 'other world'."

This entire popular dimension of archaeology should not be buried by traditional academic habits and the social values of the educated middle classes, which most professional archaeologists have probably grown up with. Regrettably, archaeologists themselves often have a fairly limited understanding of what an archaeologist actually is and what archaeological stories in our own society are about. I cannot help wondering whether non-archaeologists know better what the subject is all about than most of its professionals do. In short, archaeologists are often rather clueless about the most important dimension of archaeology in popular culture: archaeo-appeal.

Birka near Stockholm: a great archaeological day out

The Viking Age town of Birka on the island of Björkö in Lake Mälaren near Stockholm is probably the single best known archaeological site in Sweden.[62] Ever since the large-scale excavations in the early 1990s, which had been sponsored by the company TetraPak, the site and its archaeology have been receiving extensive attention in all the Swedish media (Petersson 1994). Since then, a typical question to a Swedish archaeologist has been: "Did you dig at Birka?" (Welinder 2000: 52).

In a recent survey (André et al 2001: 177), half of the sample living in Stockholm said that they had visited Birka in recent years. "Sweden's first town" is also a destination for foreign tourists visiting Stockholm, not the least because it combines a pleasant trip on the lake with the international appeal of the Vikings. During the four and a half months long season, the site is visited every year by more than 50,000 people – with the capacity of circa 300 passengers on the boat from Stockholm sometimes insufficient during the holiday period. Birka, which is managed by the Swedish National Heritage Board, has been a World Heritage Site since 1993.

[62] http://www.raa.se/birka

Although it is possible to arrive on the island in your own boat, practically all visitors come by one of the commercially-run boats leaving from various places around Lake Mälaren. The most popular trip is run by *Strömma Kanalbolaget* from Stockholm city centre. During the nearly two-hour long journey, guides hired by *Strömma* use the boat's public address system to point out archaeological sites which the boat passes and to teach all passengers some basics about the Viking Age. They also offer children's activities including writing your name in runes and dressing in Viking Age clothes. The guides are wearing uniforms supplied by the boat company, but in 2004 the style changed from fieldwork wear to Viking wear.

Once you arrive on the island in the late morning, the Birka experience typically consists of a guided tour (in Swedish or English) to the archaeological sights of the island, including a glance at the summer-time excavations, followed by a leisurely stroll on the island at your own pace, a visit to the museum and at some point a picnic or restaurant visit, before the boat takes you back. At 245 kr (£18, 27 Euros) per adult (including guided tours and museum entry but excluding food), this day trip from Stockholm is not cheap, especially if an entire family is travelling, as is often the case. But provided the weather is satisfactory, recent surveys as well as the look on the faces of the passengers on the return boat trip suggests that the experience is highly appreciated and the trip generally considered worth the money.

One of the positive aspects of this trip is the self-contained character of the day, with the moments when visitors enter and leave the boat marking beginning and end of their adventure into the past. On the island, the archaeological sites in the landscape, the ongoing excavations and the museum with associated activities, such as a Viking Age camp during high season, provide a fair number of attractions to fill the four hours between the boat's arrival and departure without anybody needing to rush. Visitors will even have time for a meal and perhaps a rest on the (poor) little beach.

When I talked to Magnus Krantz of *Strömma*, it became clear that they do not see themselves as being in the business of ferrying people across water but in the business of providing customers with experiences that incorporate boat journeys. They see each day trip in its entirety and understand that their customers expect engaging archaeological experiences during the visit to Birka. The role of the guides is crucial, for it is them who take the visitors through the different stages of the entire day. *Strömma* also appreciates that in order to make sufficient people want to visit and re-visit the island more is needed than nature, a museum and a restaurant. That is why they have been making substantial contributions to Stockholm University's new excavations which are explained to the appreciative visitors either by the guides or, once a day, by the archaeologists themselves. Since visitor numbers have been going down in recent years, *Strömma* is keen to provide additional attractions such as reconstructions of Viking Age buildings or a long-term project gradually constructing a Viking Age boat. They also began offering performed tours during which two Viking Age characters and an archaeologist ("we are like detectives") guide visitors on the island.

The Swedish National Heritage Board, formally co-operating with *Strömma*, concentrated its activities on ensuring that visitors receive academically sound, factual information about the island's past, for example through various educational materials, guide books and a museum exhibition showing finds from the island as well as models of Birka during the Viking Age. Inaddition, they have been insisting that *Strömma*'s guides, who tend to be university students, attend a special course and have certain minimum qualifications in archaeology. Approved guides, now usually wearing Viking Age costumes, display a name badge stating that they are authorised by the National Heritage Board.

In my view, the Board has not yet fully appreciated the unique opportunity to be able to engage large numbers of interested visitors over several hours during which they cannot 'escape' from the island. Although *Strömma* prefers the Viking Age as its main theme, any of the four themes discussed in chapter 5 might be used to tell exciting stories about archaeology, too. As the Swedish archaeologist Bodil Petersson showed in a study entitled *Indiana Jones on Birka* (1994), much of the reporting about Birka in the Swedish media has long been reflecting the popular interest in evocative narratives about archaeology. Celebrating archaeological stories about heroic adventures in exotic places, detectives investigating profound mysteries, large revelations to be made and professionals rescuing invaluable sites and artefacts for the future could make the visit to Birka an even more memorable adventure than it is already now. At the same time, such explicit celebrations of archaeology would provide opportunities to critique some of the problems contained both in the archaeological stereotypes being used and in the popular clichés of Birka – "Sweden's first town" that was, of course, neither really Swedish nor a real town.

At the end of the day, most of professional archaeology is not in the business of education but in storytelling. Archaeologists, like others who have tales to tell about the past, are "sophisticated storytellers" and as such they are "performers on a public stage" (Fagan 2002: 254). Archaeological stories – whether popular or strictly academic – are often hero stories where the archaeologist/hero "goes to a dangerous place and rescues something valuable" (Little 2000: 10). That is not to say that archaeology was any less important, quite the opposite. As discussed in chapter 6, appropriate stories educate people and can create political goodwill. What is more, archaeological stories can be told by many people and everybody can be given the opportunity to express their own perspectives about archaeology.

Storytelling and the emphasising of "experiences" have become central to the society in which we live. Besides their other functions, they contribute to peoples' social identities and can give inspiration, meaning and happiness to their lives (Schulze 1993; Jensen 1999). These are no small achievements – not only because of the

immediate satisfaction gained by the individuals directly affected (Fowler 1977: 28-29). Arguably, society too benefits from citizens who occasionally fulfil their dreams, can overcome adversities, develop inquiring minds, ask – and learn to deal with – large existential questions, or gain a sense of purpose from being able to contribute to important missions. If all that can be fun too, then so much for the better.

> "In explaining why she climbed over the temple's delicate rooftops, one Canadian tourist [at Preah Khan, Cambodia] explained it made her 'feel like Lara Croft exploring the jungled ruins of Angkor'."
>
> Tim Winter (2002: 334)

There is, of course, a political dimension to everything discussed in this book – not just the specific politics involved in all "public" archaeology but also the general politics concerning archaeology's role in society. It is a legitimate concern at the end of this book that archaeology may have little else to offer people other than temporary escapes from the 'real' world. As enjoyable and indeed necessary as they can be occasionally, there may be a risk that such escapes merely compensate for some of the deficiencies of peoples' real lives and thus keep them from addressing these deficiencies and ultimately trying to improve their lives. However, as I hope to have shown in this book, rather than distracting from 'reality', adventures and other kinds of stories and

experiences are very much part of the contemporary world. Arguably, they are also playing an important role in maintaining a given social order by reaffirming crucial underlying concepts and values. Moreover, as the German anthropologist Christoph Köck (1990: 160; my translation) argued, "if the transgression of boundaries were not domesticated, the existence of the [cultural] order as a whole would be at risk." In other words, temporary escapes are necessary in order to retain the *status quo* of a society in which people generally live well. But

145

not all societies provide generally good lives for their citizens and probably no social order is as good as it might be.

Nothing I said should hold professional archaeologists and others back from problematizing and critiquing the stories and themes that are associated with the subject of archaeology. Instead, a critical assessment of the audiences' interpretations and possible implications and consequences of particular meanings of archaeology are a social duty of archaeologists, too. This is the one reservation without which archaeological stories, however popular, should never be told. Such an assessment could lead to an acceptance, a required modification or a complete rejection of a particular way of depicting archaeology. Moreover, even the implications and consequences of defining archaeology as a 'brand' need to be carefully considered. As much as an academic discipline can learn from the realm of economics there are also serious downsides that make a critical attitude indispensable (see Klein 2001). Yet critical assessments are never easy and there are no general rules that could suggest perfect responses to all eventualities. Each situation needs to be looked at carefully in its entire context and must be assessed on its own merits. What makes general recommendations harder still is that everybody may have a different set of values or criteria to be applied in any such assessment.

A critique of the Nova TV documentary *Lost King of the Maya* (2001)

"The Nova production gives knowledge, expertise, and voice to leading archaeologists, and it shows North American archaeology students handling scientific surveying equipment – but the local laborers, many of them Maya, are shown with only trowel and shovel, completely voiceless. This quasi-class structure again grants agency and knowledge only to North American 'scientists' and denies it to the local people who have most at stake economically and politically.

This glorification of archaeological 'discovery' and solution to 'mysteries' will probably go a long way to attract funding to pursue more such archaeological activity, and this payoff may make the distortions and inaccuracies of a public broadcasting production seem no more than a necessary evil. But, many would argue, there is an unexpressed cost in the presentation of such colonialist hierarchies, and this is the impact the cultivation of public opinion can have on the political and economic conditions of contemporary Maya peoples – not only those living in Mexico, Guatemala, Belize, Honduras, and El Salvador, but also those forced to flee to the United States and Canada...."

Marvin Cohodas (email sent to Nova, 21 February 2001)[63]

[63] http://ethical.arts.ubc.ca/Nova.html

If I were to apply my own set of values, it would be possible to modify the existing clichés so that archaeology can still benefit from their appeal while at the same time avoiding some of their problems. For example, the A theme may have colonial and gender-related overtones that I would not want to promote in contemporary Western society. But it is possible to remove them, or parody them, and still let archaeologists participate in hero adventure stories, for their essential characteristics do not exclusively depend on these traits (see also Cohodas 2003). Similarly, as scholarly experts caring for antiquities, archaeologists adhere to the C theme, but as far as I am concerned that does not necessarily mean that in times of war they need to get embedded in the war machineries of a military superpower in order to try and protect archaeological sites. Rather, archaeologists could adjust the C theme to a commitment of caring first and foremost for human beings and thus avoid contributing to making brutal wars more feasible (see also Hamilakis 2003). Political choices such as these are ours to make.

Ending

As I am completing this chapter in September 2004, an email message from Lucy at the BBC reached my inbox:

> "I am developing new programmes for BBC history and archaeology, we have a new series we are hoping to get funding to film in 2005. The series is looking for archaeological digs at major sites where a team of researchers are trying to solve a mystery. We propose bringing together the skills of traditional archaeologists with specialists to help solve these mysteries. Specialisms might include ground-penetrating radar, aerial surveying, DNA and forensic specialists, robotics, underwater archaeology – depending on what is required at the site in order to solve a particular mystery. We are looking for major sites of ancient civilisations such as Incas, Egyptians, Romans, Aztecs, Khmer, Persians, Olmecs, Mayans, Xi'an and so on. We are hoping to shed light on sites with big name recognition such as Saqqara, Machu Picchu, Angkor Wat, Tikal, Pompeii, Herculaneum. We need a clear mystery that the team hope to solve by bringing together experts from a range of specializations (which we can help bring to the project). We are looking for digs going ahead in 2005 and need to act quickly to get permissions in place. We realise it may be difficult to dig at the most famous sites such as Machu Picchu, but perhaps there are digs going on which could shed light on

these most famous places, or techniques that have never been used before at the big sites.

Best wishes,
Lucy"

Yes! This time let us not complain about all the clichés in Lucy's proposal and let's not insist that professional archaeology is really not like this at all. Let us not patronise either her or anybody else. Instead, let us just go for it and try to make this series happen, for it is good to see that archaeology is in demand on TV. Let us celebrate the public understanding of archaeology, with Lucy and all the others at our side.

Appendix: Main Popular Culture References

Excluding web pages, which are cited in footnotes and anything produced within the context of professional archaeology (with a few exceptions).

Destinations

Archaeological Resource Centre, York, U.K.

Archaeological State Museum (Archäologisches Landesmuseum), Konstanz, Germany

Birka, near Stockholm, Sweden

British Museum, London, U.K.

Cerne Giant, Cerne Abbas, U.K.

Chessington World of Adventures, U.K.

Disney theme parks, Los Angeles, USA + Paris, France

Flag Fen, Peterborough, U.K.

Jorvik, York, U.K.

Kalkriese Museum, Kalkriese, Germany

Museum of National Antiquities (Historiska museet), Stockholm, Sweden

Mystery Park, Interlaken, Switzerland

Södra Råda, excavation project, Sweden

Events

Archaeology Day

Big Dig (Time Team, 2003)

Shops

Fine Art + Graphics Shop, Peterborough, U.K.

Past Times chain, U.K.

Games + toys

Call of Cthulhu (1981–)

Cardcaptor Sakura

Indiana Jones and the Emperor's Tomb

Lego *Adventurer* toys

Lost Cities (1999)

149

Riddle of the Sphinx **(2000)**
The Mystery of the Mummy **(2003)**
Time Detectives **online game**
Tomb Raider **games**
Tropico: Paradise Island **(2002)**

<u>Movies</u>
Carry On Behind **(1975)**
Deceived **(1991)**
Den ofrivilliga golfaren **(1991)**
Indiana Jones and the Last Crusade **(1989)**
Indiana Jones and the Temple of Doom **(1984)**
King Solomon's Mines **(1950)**
Lara Croft: Tomb Raider **(2001)**
Lara Croft Tomb Raider: The Cradle of Life **(2003)**
Liebe auf den ersten Blick **(1991)**
March or Die **(1977)**
Pascali's Island **(1988)**
Pimpernel Smith **(1941)**
Planet of the Apes **(1967)**
Raiders of the Lost Ark **(1981)**
Secret of the Incas **(1954)**
Stargate **(1994)**
Summer Lovers **(1982)**
The Adventures of Justine **(1995-6)**
The Body **(2001)**
The Mummy **films**
The Purple Rose of Cairo **(1985)**
Undiscovered Tomb **(2002)**

<u>TV channels</u>
Discovery Channel
History Channel
National Geographic Channel

TV series

Animal, Vegetable, Mineral **(1952-59)**
Ape to Man **(2005)**
C 14 – Advances into the Past (C 14 – Vorstoß in die Vergangenheit) **(1992-)**
Countries, Humans, Adventures (Länder, Menschen, Abenteuer) **(1975-)**
Digging for the Truth **(2006-)**
Extreme Archaeology **(2003-)**
Great Excavations **(2000)**
Legends of the Hidden Temple **(Nickelodeon, 1993-6)**
Nova TV: Ice Mummies **(1997)**; *Lost King of the Maya* **(2001)**
Reflections of the past (Speglingar av det förflutna) **(1996)**
Relic Hunter **(1999-2002)**
Schliemann's Heirs (Schliemann's Erben) **(1996-)**
Stargate SG-1 **(1997-)**
Star Trek **(1966-)**
Terra X **(1982-)**
The cradle of the Svea state (Svearikets Vagga) **(1981-2)**
The Excavators (Utgrävarna) **(2005)**
Time Team **(1993-)**
We are History **(2000-1)**
Wulff & Morgenthaler **(2005)**

Videos/DVDs

Grime Team **I+II (2000, 2002)**
Inca Mummies: Secrets of a Lost Empire **(2002)**

Magazines

Abenteuer Archäologie
Archaeology
British Archaeology
National Geographic Magazine
Trench One (*Time Team*)

Songs

The Who: *Dig*

Authors

Bibby, Geoffrey (1917-2001)
Burenhult, Göran (1942-)
Ceram, C.W. (= Kurt W. Marek, 1915-1972)
Connor, Beverly (1948-)
Drößler, Rudolf (1934-)
Graichen, Gisela (1944-)
Hillerman, Tony (1925-)
Peters, Elizabeth (= Barbara Mertz, 1927-)
Pörtner, Rudolf (1912-2001)
Vandenberg, Philipp (= Hans D. Hartel, 1941-)

Specific fiction

Cannon, Deborah (2004) *The Raven's Pool*
Christie, Agatha (1936) *Murder in Mesopotamia*
Drabble, Margaret (1975) *The Realms of Gold*
Frischmuth, Barbara (1980) *Bindungen*
Hawes, James (2001) *Dead Long Enough*
Innes, Hammond (1973) *Levkas Man*
Jenkins, Richard (1998) *The Archaeologist*
Jersild, P. C. (2003) *De ondas kloster*
Macaulay, David (1979), *Motel of the Mysteries*
McCaffrey, Anne and Mercedes Lackey (1992) *The Ship Who Searched.*
McDevitt, Jack (2001) *Deepsix*
Mitchell, Julian (1977) *Half-Life*
Mårtenson, Jan (1996) *Caesars örn*
Pachinko, Joe (1997) *Swamp!*
Peters, Ellis (1973) *City of Gold and Shadows*
Ripley, Mike (2002) *Angel Underground*
Traxler, Hans (1983) *Die Wahrheit über Hänsel und Gretel*
Vardeman, Robert (1989) *Weapons of Chaos*
Wirsén, Carin + Stina Wirsén (2000) *Rut & Knut gräver ut*

Specific non-fiction

Ceram, C. W. (1949) *Götter, Gräber und Gelehrte* (*Gods, Graves and Scholars*).
Diamond, Jared (2005) *Collapse*

Ryan, Donald (1999) *The Complete Idiot's Guide to Lost Civilizations*
Time Life book series on *Lost Civilizations*

Characters
Alex West (*Lara Croft: Tomb Raider*)
Amelia Peabody (*Elizabeth Peters novels*)
Berglund, state archaeologist (*Den ofrivilliga golfaren*)
Daniel Jackson (*Stargate*)
Dr Elsa Schneider (*Indiana Jones and the Last Crusade*)
Erich von Däniken (1935-)
Frances Wingate (*The Realms of Gold*)
Fujitaka Kinomoto, aka Aiden Avalon (*Cardcaptor Sakura*)
Heinrich Schliemann (1822-1890)
Howard Carter (1874-1939)
Indiana Jöns (*Donald Duck*)
Jean-Luc Picard (*Star Trek*)
King Gustav VI Adolf (1882-1973)
Lara Croft
Martin Mystère
Phil Harding (*Time Team*) (late 1940s-)
Professor Bernice Summerfield (*Doctor Who*)
Professor Glyn Daniel (1914-1986)
Professor Henry Jones
Professor Hercules Taragon (*Tintin*)
Professor Indiana Jones
Professor Jeffrey Fairbrother (*Hi-De-Hi*)
Professor Kilroy (*Lego*)
Professor Lucien Kastner + Sir Robert Eversley (*Monty Python's Flying Circus*)
Professor Mick Aston (*Time Team*) (1946-)
Professor Robson (*The Adventures of Justine*)
Professor Roland Crump (*Carry On Behind*)
Professor Sydney Fox (*Relic Hunter*)
Professor William Harper Littlejohn (*Doc Savage*)
Rick Dangerous
Sir Mortimer Wheeler (1890-1976)
Tom Baxter (*The Purple Rose of Cairo*)

Cornelius Holtorf

Tony Robinson (*Time Team*) (1946–)
Vash (*Star Trek*)
Will Rock

References

Adams, William (1973) The Archaeologist as Detective. In: D. Lathrap and J. Douglas (eds) *Variation in Anthropology*, pp. 17-29. Urbana: Illinois Archaeological Survey.

Addyman, Peter (1987) Perception and presentation of the past: scholarly significance and public benefit. Paper given at a conference held at the University of Minneapolis, October 1987.

Addyman, Peter (1990) Reconstruction as interpretation: the example of the Jorvik Viking Centre, York. In: P. Gathercole and D. Lowenthal (eds) *The Politics of the Past*, pp.257-264. London: Routledge.

Agenda Kulturarv (2004) *Människan i centrum. Agenda Kulturarvs programförklaring.* Stockholm. Also at http://ux-ra-kmsap2.raa.se/opencms/export/agendakulturarv// dokument/Arkiv/Programforklaring/Slutver.PF.pdf.

André, Anna Maria, Karolin Dahlén, Mikael Grexing, Josefina Lif, Pia Linde, Anneli Lövgren, Gundborg Mellergård, Åsa Nathanaelsson, Kristin Söderlund, Stig Welinder and Helena Åberg (2001) Arkeologi och kulturmiljövård. Vad och varför? *Fornvännen* 96, 177-180.

Andreae, Bernard Ed. (1981) *Archäologie und Gesellschaft: Forschung und öffentliches Interesse.* Stuttgart: Wissenschaftliche Verlagsgesellschaft.

Aronsson, Peter and Erika Larsson Eds. (2002) *Konsten att lära och viljan att uppleva. Historiebruk och upplevelsepedagogik vid Foteviken, Medeltidsveckan och Jamtli.* Växjö University: Centre for Cultural Studies.

Ascher, Robert (1960) Archaeology and the public image. *American Antiquity* 25, 402-403.

Ascherson, Neal (2004) Archaeology and the British Media. In: N. Merriman (ed.) *Public Archaeology*, pp. 145-158. London and New York: Routledge.

Atkinson, Paul (1996) *Sociological Readings and Re-readings*. Aldershot et al: Avebury.

Bahn, Paul (1989) *Bluff your way in Archaeology*. Horsham: Ravette.

Baxter, Jane (2002a) Popular images and popular stereotypes. Images of archaeologists in popular and documentary film. *The SAA Archaeological Record* 2 (4), 16-17, 40. http://www.saa.org/Publications/thesaaarchrec/sep02.pdf.

Baxter, Jane (2002b) Teaching with 'Indie': Using Film and Television to Teach Archaeology. *The SAA Archaeological Record* 2 (5), 18-20. http://www.saa.org/Publications/thesaaarchrec/nov02.pdf.

Benz, Marion and Liedmeier, Anna K. (forthcoming) The German press and archaeology. In: T. Clack and M. Brittain (eds) *The Media's Past: Archaeology in Contemporary Popular Culture*. London: UCL Press.

Beth, Thomas and Karlheinz Steinmüller (2004) The natural sciences caught between publicity and science fiction. A conversation with Stefan Iglhaut and Thomas Spring. In: *Science + Fiction. Between Nanoworlds and Glocla Culture*, pp. 233-249. Berlin: Jovis.

Betty, Peter K. (2002) Anyone for writing? *Antiquity* 76, 1054-8.

Bjorklund, Diana (2001) Sociologists as characters in twentieth-century novels. *The American Sociologist* 32 (4), 23-41.

Bohne, Anke and Marcus U. Heinrich (2000) Das Bild der Archäologie in der Öffentlichkeit. Eine Befragung in Bonn und Köln. *Mitteilungen des Deutschen Archäologen-Verbandes e.V.* 31(2), 1-34.

Borbein, Adolf (1981) Archäologie und historisches Bewußtsein. In: B. Andreae (ed.) *Archäologie und Gesellschaft: Forschung und öffentliches Interesse*, pp. 45-76. Stuttgart: Wissenschaftliche Verlagsgesellschaft.

Bray, Warwick (1981) Archaeological Humour: The Private Joke and the Public Image. In: J. Evans, B. Cunliffe and C. Renfrew (eds) *Antiquity and Man. Essays in Honour of Glyn Daniel*, pp. 221-229. London: Thames and Hudson.

Broadbent, Noel (2004) The Ethics of Collaborative Research in Sweden. Finding common ground with local and indigenous people. In: H. Karlsson (ed.) *Swedish Archaeologists on Ethics*, pp. 87-98. Göteborg: Bricoleur.

Burenhult, Göran (1975) Arkeologi – för vem? *Fornvännen 70*, 238-40.

Burenhult, Göran (1986) *Speglingar av det förflutna*. Höganäs: Bra Böcker.

Burström, Mats (2004) Archaeology and Existential Reflection. In: H. Bolin (ed.) *The Interplay of Past and Present*, pp. 20-28.

Byrne, Denis (1995) Buddhist *stupa* and Thai social practice. *World Archaeology 27*, 266-281.

Campbell, Joseph (1988) *The Hero With a Thousand Faces* [1949]. London: Fontana.

Cannon, Deborah (2004) *The Raven's Pool*. Victoria, BC: Trafford.

Ceram, C. W. (1980) *Gods, Graves and Scholars: the Story of Archaeology* [first published in German in 1949]. Harmondsworth: Penguin.

Cleere, Henry (1988) Whose Archaeology is it anyway? In: J. Bintliff (ed) *Extracting Meaning from the Past*, pp. 37-43. Oxford: Oxbow.

Cleere, Henry (2000) Review of T. Taylor [1998] Behind the Scenes at Time Team. London. *Public Archaeology 1*, 90-2.

Cohodas, Marvin (2003) A New Heroics of Archaeology. Paper presented at the Fifth World Archaeological Congress, Washington, DC in June 2003.

Cole, John (1980) Cult Archaeology and Unscientific Method and Theory. *Advances in Archaeological Method and Theory* 3, 1-33.

Daniel, Glyn (1964) *The Idea of Prehistory* [1962]. Harmondsworth: Penguin.

Däniken, Cornelia v. and Erich v. Däniken (2005) *Der Mystery Park. Die Geschichte, die Menschen.* Interlaken: Mystery Park.

Darvill, Tim (2004) Archaeology in rock. In: N. Brodie and C. Hills (eds) *Material engagements: studies in honour of Colin Renfrew*, pp. 55-77. Cambridge: McDonald Institute for Archaeological Research.

Darvill, Tim, Katherine Barker, Barbara Bender and Ronald Hutton (1999) *The Cerne Giant. An antiquity on trial.* Oxford: Oxbow.

Day, David (1997) *A Treasure Hard to Attain. Images of Archaeology in Popular Film, with a Filmography.* Lanham and London: Scarecrow Press.

de Boer, Trent (2004) *Shovel Bum. Comix of Archaeological Field Life.* Walnut Creek etc: Altamira.

Denning, Kathryn (1999) Apocalypse past/future. Archaeology and folklore, writ large. In: C. Holtorf and A. Gazin-Schwartz (eds) *Archaeology and Folklore*, pp. 90-105. London and New York: Routledge.

Derks, Heidrun (2003) Kalkriese – oder: wie man eine Schlacht ausstellt. *Archäologische Informationen* 26, 127-132.

Diamond, Jared (2005) *Collapse: How Societies Choose to Fail or Succeed.* London: Penguin.

Elam, Mark and Margareta Bertilsson (2003) Consuming, Engaging and Confronting Science: The Emerging Dimensions of Scientific Citizenship. *European Journal of Social Theory* 6, 233-251.

English Heritage (2000) *Attitudes towards the Heritage.* Research Study Conducted for English Heritage, July 2000. http://www.english-heritage.org.uk/default.

asp?wci=WebItem&WCE=158 (accessed 28 September 2004).

Fagan, Brian (2002) Epilogue. In: B. Little (ed) *Public Benefits of Archaeology*, pp. 253-60. Gainesville etc.: University Press of Florida.

Felder, Kathrin, Isabella Hammer, Juliane Lippok and Mareile Wulf (2003) Erkenntnisgewinn und Unterhaltungswert – eine Analyse von Archäologiebildern in den Unterhaltungsmedien. *Ethnographisch-Archäologische Zeitschrift* 44, 161-182.

Fowler, Peter (1977) *Approaches to Archaeology*. London: Adam and Charles Black.

Frank, Scott (2003) Reel Reality: Science Consultants in Hollywood. *Science as Culture* 12, 427-69.

French, Michael (n.d.). Tomb Raiders: The Idea of the Adventurer. http://www.theraider. net/features/articles/tomb_raiders.php.

Fritz, John M. (1973) Relevance, Archaeology and Subsistence Theory. In: C. Redman (ed) *Research and Theory in Current Archaeology*, pp. 59-82. New York: Wiley & Sons.

Gamble, Clive (2001) *Archaeology. The Basics*. London and New York: Routledge.

Gerbner, George (1987) Science on television: how it affects public conceptions. *Issues in Science and Technology* Spring 1987, 109-115.

Gero, Joan and Dolores Root (1990) Public Presentations and Private Concerns: Archeology in the Pages of the National Geographic. In: P. Gathercole and D. Lowenthal (eds) *The Politics of the Past*, pp. 19-37. London: Unwin Hyman.

Gowlett, John (1990) Indiana Jones: crusading for archaeology? Review of S. Spielberg (dir.), Indiana Jones and the Last Crusade. *Antiquity* 64, 157.

Graichen, Gisela (1993) Tagebuch der Antike. In: G. Graichen and H. H. Hillrichs (eds) *C 14 – Die Gebeine des Papstes. Neue archäologische Entdeckungen in Deutschland*, pp. 11-14. München: Bertelsmann.

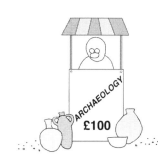

Graichen, Gisela (1995) 'Time-digger' oder die Entschlüsselung von Botschaften aus einer anderen Welt. In: G. Graichen and M. Siebler (eds) *Schliemanns Erben. Entschlüsseln Archäologen unsere Zukunft?*, pp. 11-23. Mainz: Zabern.

- "...now that I've read all those I haven't got the energy for practical archaeology"

Graichen, Gisela (1999) Vorstoß in die Vergangenheit. In: G. Graichen and H. H. Hillrichs (eds) *C 14. Vorstoß in die Vergangenheit. Archäologische Entdeckungen in Deutschland* [1992], pp. 12-18. München: Goldmann.

Graichen, Gisela and Hans Helmut Hillrichs Eds (1999) *C 14. Vorstoß in die Vergangenheit. Archäologische Entdeckungen in Deutschland* [1992]. München: Goldmann.

Gregory, Jane and Steve Miller (1998) *Science in Public. Communication, Culture, and Credibility.* New York and London: Plenum.

Gründel, Achim and Helmut Ziegert (1983) Archäologie und Kriminalistik. Ziele und Wege der Erkenntnisgewinnung. *Archäologische Informationen* 5, 175-192.

Gustafsson, Anders and Håkan Karlsson (2004) *Plats på scen. Kring beskrivning och förmedling av Bohusläns fasta fornlämningar genom tiderna.* Uddevalla: Bohuslän's Museum.

Hall, Mark (2004) Romancing the stones: archaeology in popular cinema. *European Journal of Archaeology* 7, 159-76.

Hamilakis, Yannis (2003) Iraq, stewardship and the "record": An ethical crisis for archaeology. *Public Archaeology* 3, 104-111. Available at http://www.arch.soton.ac.uk/Research/yannis/hamilakis.pdf.

Hargreaves, Ian and Galit Ferguson (2000) *Who's misunderstanding whom? Bridging the gulf of understanding between the public, the media and science.* Report published on behalf of the Economic and Social Research Council. http://web.archive.org/web/20041024070349/http://www.esrc.ac.uk/esrccontent/PublicationsList/whom/whofirst.html.

Hawes, James (2001) *Dead Long Enough* [2000]. London: Vintage.

Haynes, Roslynn (1994) *From Faust to Strangelove. Representations of the Scientist in Western Literature.* Baltimore and London: Johns Hopkins University Press.

Healey, Peter (1999) Popularising science for the sake of the economy: the UK experience. In: R. Miettinen (ed) *Biotechnology and Public Understanding of Science*, pp. 68-81. Helsinki: Edita.

Hendriks, Suzanne (2005) De Indiana Jones-Factor. De onvermijdelijkheid van de romantische held in populair-wetenschappelijke archeologische documentaires. Unpublished Masters thesis, University of Amsterdam.

Hills, Catherine (2003) What is television doing for us? Reflections on some recent British programmes. *Antiquity* 77, 206-211.

Hoffman, Teresa (1997) The Role of Public Participation: Arizona's Public Archaeology Program. In: J. Jameson, Jr. (ed) *Presenting Archaeology to the Public. Digging for Truths*, pp. 73-83. Walnut Creek etc.: Altamira Press.

Högberg, Anders (2004) Bilder av skånsk uppdragsarkeologi hos allmänheten och i dagspress. *META* 2004/4, 40-55.

Holmgren, Richard and Anders Kaliff (2003) *Arkeologer i Bibelns Sodom.* Stockholm: Wahlström & Widstrand.

Holtorf, Cornelius (2000) Paul Feyerabend. Towards a Democratic Relativism in Archaeology (with comments by Kathryn Denning and Per Cornell). In: C. Holtorf and H. Karlsson (eds) *Philosophy and Archaeological Practice*, pp. 241-59. Göteborg: Bricoleur Press.

Holtorf, Cornelius (2004) Doing archaeology in popular culture. In: H. Bolin (ed.) *The Interplay of Past and Present*, pp. 40-48. Huddinge: Södertörns högskola.

Holtorf, Cornelius (2005) *From Stonehenge to Las Vegas. Archaeology as Popular Culture.* Walnut Creek: Altamira Press.

House of Lords (2000) *Science and Society.* Third Report of the Science and Technology Committee, Session 1999-2000. London: House of Lords. http://www.publications.parliament.uk/pa/ld199900/ldselect/ldsctech/38/3801.htm.

Hunter, John (1996) A background to forensic archaeology. In: J. Hunter, C. Roberts and A. Martin (eds) *Studies in Crime: An Introduction to Forensic Archaeology*, pp. 7-23. London: Batsford.

Innes, Hammond (1973) *Levkas Man* [1971]. London: Fontana.

Jenkins, Richard (1998) *The Archaeologist.* London: Citron.

Jensen, Inken and Alfried Wieczorek Eds (2002) *Dino, Zeus und Asterix. Zeitzeuge Archäologie in Werbung, Kunst und Alltag heute.* Mannheim: Reiss-Engelhorn-Museen and Langenweißbach: Beier & Beran.

Jensen, Rolf (1999) *The Dream Society. How the coming shift from information to imagination will transform your business.* New York: McGraw-Hill.

Jensen, Rolf (2002) Storytelling in management, marketing and advertising. Paper available at http://www.dreamcompany.dk/en/contribution/articles.php?id=4 (accessed 2 September 2004).

Jones, Kevin and Julie M. Longstreth (2002) Pursuing the ZiNj Strategy Like There's No Tomorrow. In: B. Little (ed.) *Public Benefits of Archaeology*, pp. 187-192. Gainesville etc: University Press of Florida.

Jordan, Paul (1981) Archaeology and Television. In: J. Evans, B. Cunliffe and C. Renfrew (eds) *Antiquity and Man. Essays in Honour of Glyn Daniel*, pp. 207-213. London: Thames and Hudson.

Källén, Anna (2004) Elusive Spirits and/or Precious Phosphates. On archaeological knowledge production at Lao Pako. In: H. Karlsson (ed.) *Swedish Archaeologists on Ethics*, pp. 99-116. Göteborg: Bricoleur.

Kapff, Dieter (2004) Journalisten und Archäologie. Gedanken zum Stellenwert der Archäologie und der Zusammenarbeit von Wissenschaft und Presse. *Archäologisches Nachrichtenblatt* 9, 127-30.

Karlsson, Catarina (2004) *Arkeologi- och kommunikationsprojektet i Södra Råda 2003*. Örebro: Swedish National Heritage Board, UV Bergslagen. Available at http://www.raa.se/uv/sodrarada/pdf/kommunikationsrapport2004_5_72.pdf.

Karlsson, Håkan and Björn Nilsson (2000) *Arkeologins publika relation. En kritisk rannsakning*. Göteborg: Bricoleur.

Kidder, Alfred (1949) Introduction. In: C. Amsden, *Prehistoric Southwesterners from Basketmaker to Pueblo*, pp. XI-XIV. Los Angeles: Southwest Museum.

Kirby, David (2003) Science Consultants, Fictional Films, and Scientific Practice. *Social Studies of Science* 33, 231-268.

Kirchner, Horst (1964) Die Archäologie im Geschichtsbild der Gegenwart. Gedanken zu repräsentativen Stimmen der Zeit. *Jahrbuch des Römisch-Germanischen Zentralmuseums Mainz* 11, 1-14.

Klein, Naomi (2001) *No Logo*. London: Flamingo.

Köck, Christoph (1990) *Sehnsucht Abenteuer. Auf den Spuren der Erlebnisgesellschaft*. Berlin: Transit.

Kohl, Philip and Clare Fawcett Eds (1995) *Nationalism, politics and the practice of archaeology.* Cambridge: Cambridge University Press.

Kulik, Karol (2003a) Same Story, Different Spin? British National Press Coverage of the 1998 Hominid Discovery in Sterkfontein, South Africa. Unpublished manuscript.

Kulik, Karol (2003b) British TV Archaeology and the Public. Unpublished manuscript.

Lagerqvist, Lars and Maj Odelberg (1972) *Kungen gräver. En bok om arkeologer och arkeologi.* Stockholm: Askild & Kärnekull and Statens historiska museum.

Little, Barbara (1991) Popular Culture, Material Culture: Some Archaeological Thoughts. In: R. Browne and P. Browne (eds) *Digging into Popular Culture,* pp. 25-35. Bowling Green, Ohio: Bowling Green State University Popular Press.

Little, Barbara (2000) Compelling Images Through Storytelling. *Historical Archaeology* 34, 10-13.

Löfgren, Orvar (1999) *On Holiday. A History of Vacationing.* Berkeley: University of California Press.

Lucas, Gavin (2004) Modern Disturbances: On the Ambiguities of Archaeology. *Modernism/modernity* 11, 109-120. Available at http://muse.jhu.edu/journals/modernism-modernity/v011/11.1lucas.pdf

Maase, Kaspar (2003) Selbstfeier und Kompensation. Zum Studium der Unterhaltung. In: K. Maase and B. J. Warneken (eds) *Unterwelten der Kultur. Themen und Theorien der volkskundlichen Kulturwissenschaft,* pp. 219-242. Köln etc.: Böhlau.

Macaulay, David (1979) *The Motel of the Mysteries.* Boston: Houghton Mifflin.

MacClancy, Jeremy (2005) The literary image of anthropologists. *Journal of the Royal Anthropological Institute* (N.S.) 11, 549-575.

MacGregor, Rob (1989) *Indiana Jones and the last crusade.* London: Sphere.

Mackinney, Lisa H. (1994a) "Something Old in the Earth": Front-End Interviews about Archaeology with Visitors to the California Academy of Sciences. Unpublished report.

Mackinney, Lisa H. (1994b) "That Sense of Adventure": Front-End Interviews about Archaeology and Indiana Jones with Visitors to the California Academy of Sciences. Unpublished report.

Maier, Franz G. (1981) Archäologie und moderne Welt. In: B. Andreae (ed.) *Archäologie und Gesellschaft: Forschung und öffentliches Interesse*, pp. 31-44. Stuttgart: Wissenschaftliche Verlagsgesellschaft.

Maier-Maidl, Verena and Ingrid Stipper-Lackner (1997) Wer hat den Schenkel von Jupiter geklaut? Das Bild des klassischen Archäologen im Film. In: G. Erath, M. Lehner and G. Schwarz (eds) *KOMOS. Festschrift für Thuri Lorenz zum 65. Geburtstag*, pp. 287-289. Wien: Phoibos.

McCaffrey, Anne and Mercedes Lackey (1992) *The Ship Who Searched*. Riverdale: Baen.

Membury, Steven (2002) The Celluloid Archaeologist – an X-rated exposé. In: M. Russell (ed.) *Digging Holes in Popular Culture. Archaeology and Science Fiction*, pp. 8-18. Oxford and Oakville: Oxbow / The David Brown Book Company.

Merriman, Nick (1991) *Beyond the Glass Case. The Past, the Heritage and the Public in Britain*. Leicester, London and New York: Leicester University Press.

Merriman, Nick (2002) Archaeology, heritage and interpretation. In: B. Cunliffe, W. Davies and C. Renfrew (eds) *Archaeology. The Widening Debate*, pp. 541-566. Oxford: Oxford University Press.

Merriman, Nick (2004) Introduction: diversity and dissonance in public archaeology. In: N. Merriman (ed.) *Public Archaeology*, pp. 1-17. London and New York: Routledge.

Meyer, Jürgen (2002) *Archäologische Geheimnisse. Rätselhafte Entdeckungen zwischen Neckar und Alb*. Reutlingen: Oertel + Spörer.

Mitchell, Julian (1977) *Half-Life*. National Theatre Plays. London: Heinemann.

Cornelius Holtorf

Moore, Lawrence E. (2006) Going Public: Customization and American Archaeology. *The SAA Archaeological Record*, May 2006, 16-19.

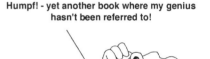

Humpf! - yet another book where my genius hasn't been referred to!

Moscovici, Serge (1984) The phenomenon of social representations. In: R. Farr and S. Moscovici (eds) *Social representations*, pp. 3-69. Cambridge: Cambridge University Press.

Moser, Stephanie (forthcoming) Gendered dimensions of archaeological practice. The stereotyping of archaeology as fieldwork. In: A. Wylie and M. Conkey (eds) *Practicing Archaeology as a Feminist*. Santa Fe, NM: School of American Research.

Norman, Bruce (1983) Archaeology and television. *Archaeological Review from Cambridge* 2 (1), 27-32.

Näsman, Ulf (1989) Populärarkeologi – förmedling och levandegörande. In: *Levandegörande arkeologi – hur och varför*, pp. 10-19. Stockholm: Swedish National Heritage Board and Statens Historiska Museer.

O'Dell, Tom Ed. (2002) *Upplevelsens materialitet*. Lund: Studentlitteratur.

Oels, David (2005) Ceram – Keller – Pörtner. Die archäologischen Bestseller der fünfziger Jahre als historischer Projektionsraum In: W. Hardtwig and E. Schütz (eds) *Geschichte für Leser. Populäre Geschichtsschreibung in Deutschland im 20. Jahrhundert*, pp. 345-370. Stuttgart: Steiner.

Opaschowski, Horst (2000) *Kathedralen des 21. Jahrhunderts. Erlebniswelten im Zeitalter der Eventkultur*. Hamburg: B.A.T. Freizeit-Forschungsinstitut.

Pachinko, Joe (1997) *Swamp!* Berkeley: Superstition Street Press.

Packard, Vance (1960) *The Hidden Persuaders* [1957]. Harmondsworth: Penguin.

Pallottino, Massimo (1968) *The Meaning of Archaeology*. London: Thames and Hudson.

Paynton, Ceinwen (2002) Public perception and 'pop archaeology': a survey of current attitudes toward televised archaeology in Britain. *The SAA Archaeological Record*, March 2002, 33-44.

Petersson, Bodil (1994) *Indiana Jones på Birka. Om arkeologisk popularisering och forskning*. Unpublished thesis (D-uppsats). Institute of Archaeology and Ancient History, University of Lund.

Picknett, Lynn and Clive Prince (2003) Alternative Egypts. In: S. MacDonald and M. Rice (eds) *Consuming Ancient Egypt*, pp. 175-93. London: UCL Press.

Pine, Joseph, II and James Gilmore (1999) *The Experience Economy. Work is Theatre & Every Business a Stage*. Boston, MA: Harvard Business School Press.

Pohl, John (1996) Archaeology in film and television. In: B. Fagan (ed) *The Oxford Companion to Archaeology*, pp. 574-5. New York and Oxford: Oxford University Press.

Pokotylo, David (2002) Public Opinion and Canadian Archaeological Heritage: A National Perspective. *Canadian Journal of Archaeology* 26, 88-129

Pokotylo, David and Andrew Mason (1991) Public attitudes towards archaeological resources and their management. In: G. Smith and J. Ehrenhard (eds) *Protecting the Past*, pp. 9-18. Boca Rato etc: CRC Press. Also published online at http://www.cr.nps.gov/seac/protecting/html/1b-pokotyl.htm.

Pokotylo, David and Neil Guppy (1999) Public opinion and archaeological heritage: views from outside the profession. *American Antiquity* 64, 400-16.

Popcorn, Faith (1992) *The Popcorn Report. Revolutionary Trend Predictions for Marketing in the 1990s* [1991]. London: Arrow.

Preston, Douglas and Lincoln Child (1999) *Thunderhead*. New York: Warner.

Pühringer, Elisabeth (2000) *Der Weg in die Urzeit. Archäologie und Film*. Unpublished Doctoral dissertation. Universität Wien.

Ramos, Maria and David Duganne (2000) *Exploring Public Perceptions and Attitudes about Archaeology*. Report by HarrisInteractive on behalf of the Society for American Archaeology. http://www.saa.org/pubedu/nrptdraft4.pdf.

Ransley, Jesse (2005) Boats are for boys: queering maritime archaeology. *World Archaeology* 37: 621-9.

Redman, Charles (1999) *Human Impact on Ancient Environments*. Tucson: University of Arizona Press.

Rieche, Anita (1996) Archäologie für jedermann – populärwissenschaftliche Schriften zu Archäologie/Bodendenkmalpflege. *Archäologisches Nachrichtenblatt* 1, 152-159.

Ripley, Mike (2002) *Angel Underground*. London: Robinson.

Robinson, Tony and Mick Aston (2002) *Archaeology is Rubbish. A Beginner's Guide*. London: Channel 4 Books.

Rose, Mark (2003) Taking a Stab at the Past. Will archaeology survive another Tomb Raider movie? *Archaeology Magazine* Online feature, posted 24 July 2003 at http://www.archaeology.org/online/reviews/tombraider/index2.html.

Russell, Miles Ed. (2002a) *Digging Holes in Popular Culture. Archaeology and Science Fiction*. Oxford and Oakville: Oxbow / The David Brown Book Company.

Russell, Miles (2002b) "No more heroes any more": the dangerous world of the pop culture archaeologist. In: M. Russell (ed.) *Digging Holes in Popular Culture. Archaeology and Science Fiction*, pp. 38-54. Oxford and Oakville: Oxbow / The David Brown Book Company.

Ryan, Donald (1999) *The Complete Idiot's Guide to Lost Civilizations.* Indianapolis: Alpha Books.

Sandberg, Catrin (2006) *Arkeologen som filmhjälte.* Unpublished C-uppsats. Department of Archaeology, University of Göteborg.

Schadla-Hall, Tim and Genny Morris (2003) Ancient Egypt on the small screen – from fact to fiction in the UK. In: S. MacDonald and M. Rice (eds) *Consuming Ancient Egypt,* pp. 195-215. London: UCL Press.

Schmidt, Martin (2000) Archaeology and the German public. In: H. Härke (ed.) *Archaeology, Ideology, and Society. The German experience,* pp. 240-270. Frankfurt/M. Etc: Lang.

Schmitt, Bernd (1999) *Experiental Marketing. How to Get Customers to Sense, Feel, Think, Act, and Relate to Your Company and Brands.* New York: The Free Press.

Schörken, Rolf (1995) *Begegnungen mit Geschichte. Vom außerwissenschaftlichen Umgang mit der Historie in Literatur und Medien.* Stuttgart: Klett-Cotta.

Schulze, Gerhard (1993) *Die Erlebnisgesellschaft. Kultursoziologie der Gegenwart* [1992]. 3rd edition. Frankfurt and New York: Campus.

Sebastian, Lynne (2003) The awful truth about archaeology. *The SAA Archaeological Record* 3 (2), 35-37. Available at http://www.saa.org/publications/theSAAarchRec/mar03.pdf.

Shepherd, Nick (2002) Heading south, looking north. Why we need a post-colonial archaeology. *Archaeological Dialogues* 9, 74-82.

Shohat, Ella and Robert Stam (1994) *Unthinking Eurocentrism. Multiculturalism and the media.* London and New York: Routledge.

Silberman, Neil A. (1999) Is Archaeology Ready for Prime Time? *Archaeology Magazine* May/June 1999, 79-82.

Smardz, Karolyn (1997) The Past Through Tomorrow: Interpreting Toronto's Heritage to a Multicultural Public. In: J. Jameson (ed.) *Presenting Archaeology to the Public. Digging for Truths*, pp. 101-113. Walnut Creek etc.: Altamira Press.

Solomon, Jon (1998) Decades of Make Believe. *Archaeology Magazine* Sept/Oct 1998, 92-95.

Staaf, Björn M. (2000) The Rise and Decline(?) of the Modern in Sweden. *Current Swedish Archaeology* 8, 179-194.

Statistiska Centralbyrån (2002) *Vad betyder kulturmiljön för dig?* http://ux-ra-kmsap2.raa.se/opencms/export/agendakulturarv//dokument/scbrapport.pdf.

Stern, Tom (2002) Weltwunder und Wunderwelten. Schliemann's Erbschaft an Indiana Jones. In: I. Jensen and A. Wieczorek (eds) *Dino, Zeus und Asterix. Zeitzeuge Archäologie in Werbung, Kunst und Alltag heute*, pp. 161-166. Mannheim: Reiss-Engelhorn-Museen and Langenweißbach: Beier & Beran.

Stern, Tom and Thomas Tode (2002) Das Bild des Archäologen in Film und Fernsehen – Eine Annäherung. In: *ARCHÄOLOGIE* virtuell. *Projekte, Entwicklungen, Tendenzen seit 1995*, pp. 71-80. Bonn: Habelt. English translation of an earlier version in: Arbeitsgruppe Film der Universität Kiel (ed.) *CINARCHEA 1998: Symposium "Archäologie und Neue Medien"*. Kiel.

Steuben, Hans von (1977) Erscheinungsformen und Motive des Publikumsinteresses an Archäologie. In: R. Kurzrock (ed.) *Archäologie*, pp. 9-17. Forschung und Information 24. Berlin: Colloquium.

Swain, Hedley (1997) Mirroring reality? Images of archaeologists. *The Archaeologist* 30, 16-7. Also available at http://www.archdiggers.co.uk/diggers/page_hedley.html.

Talalay, Lauren (2004) The past as commodity. Archaeological images in modern advertising. *Public Archaeology* 3, 205-16.

Thomas, Julian (2004) *Archaeology and Modernity*. London and New York: Routledge.

Traxler, Hans (1983) *Die Wahrheit über Hänsel und Gretel.* Reinbek: Rowohlt.

Trümpler, Charlotte Ed. (2001) *Agatha Christie and Archaeology.* London: British Museum Press.

Watrall, Ethan (2002) Digital pharaoh: Archaeology, public education and interactive entertainment. *Public Archaeology* 2, 163-169.

Weingart, Peter (1998) Science and the media. *Research Policy* 27, 869-79.

Weingart, Peter, with Claudia Muhl and Petra Pansegrau (2003) Of power maniacs and unethical geniuses: science and scientists in fiction film. *Public Understanding of Science* 12, 279-287.

Welinder, Stig (1987) *Arkeologiska bilder.* Varia, Universitets Oldsaksamling, 14. Oslo.

Welinder, Stig (1997) Arkeologi i massmedia. *Fornvännen* 92, 19-32.

Welinder, Stig (2000) *Arkeologisk yrkesidentitet.* Universitet i Tromsø, Institutt for arkeologi.

Willis, John (2001) Past is perfect. *The Guardian* 29 October 2001. http://education. guardian.co.uk/print/0,3858,4286861-108247,00.html.

Winter, Tim (2002) Angkor Meets *Tomb Raider:* setting the scene. *International Journal of Heritage Studies* 8, 323-336.

Zarmati, Louise (1995) Popular archaeology and the archaeologist as hero. In: J. Balme and W. Beck (eds) *Gendered Archaeology. The Second Australian Women in Archaeology Conference,* pp. 43-47. Canberra: ANH Publications.

Zintzen, Christiane (1998) *Von Pompeji nach Troja: Archäologie, Literatur und Öffentlichkeit im 19. Jahrhundert.* Wien: WUV Universitätsverlag.

Zorpidu, Sultana (2004) The Public Image of the Female Archaeologist. The Case of Lara Croft. In: H. Bolin (ed) *The Interplay of Past and Present,* pp. 101-107. Huddinge: Södertörns högskola.

171

Index

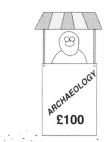

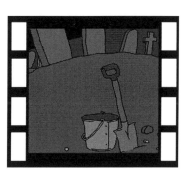

Note on the author

Cornelius Holtorf is married with two children and lives in southern Sweden. Currently an Assistant Professor in Archaeology at the University of Lund, his other books include *Archaeology and Folklore*, co-edited with A. Gazin-Schwartz (Routledge, 1999), *From Stonehenge to Las Vegas. Archaeology as Popular Culture* (Altamira, 2005) and *Contemporary Archaeologies: Excavating Now*, co-edited with Angela Piccini (Left Coast Press, 2007). He is also the Reviews Editor of the *European Journal of Archaeology* (Sage).

Note on the illustrator

Quentin Drew is not married but does have two rabbits and lives in mid-Wales. He is a Lecturer in Archaeology and the Director of Foundation Studies at the University of Wales, Lampeter. With a long catalogue of published illustrations from the past thirty years, this book sees a welcome return to cartooning.

183